BLOOMSBURY KITCHEN LIBRARY

Starters

Bloomsbury Books
London

This edition published 1995 by Bloomsbury Books,
an imprint of The Godfrey Cave Group,
42 Bloomsbury Street, London, WC1B 3QJ.

ISBN 1 85471 597 6

Printed and bound in Great Britain.

Starters

Contents

Devilled Crab

Serves 4 as
a first course

Working
(and total)
time: about
20 minutes

Calories
125

Protein
17g

Cholesterol
.85mg

Total fat
5g

Saturated fat
1g

Sodium
390mg

1	crab, dressed, brown and white meat kept separate (about 300 g/10 oz crab meat)	1
3 tbsp	plain low-fat yogurt	3 tbsp
25 g	fine fresh wholemeal breadcrumbs	¾ oz
½	lemon, finely grated rind and juice only	½
1 tsp	Dijon mustard	1 tsp
2 tsp	Worcester sauce	2 tsp
½ tsp	paprika	½ tsp
⅛ tsp	salt	⅛ tsp
½	hard-boiled egg, yolk and white separated, white finely chopped	½

Mash the white crab meat with the back of a fork to break it into separate strands, then set it aside. Place the brown crab meat in a food processor. Add the yogurt, breadcrumbs, lemon rind and juice, mustard, Worcester sauce, paprika and salt, and process to a smooth purée. Transfer the purée to a bowl, and stir in the white crab meat. Turn the crab into a serving dish.

Press the egg yolk through a sieve. Sprinkle the egg yolk and egg white over the devilled crab and serve it at room temperature.

Three-Mushroom Marinade

Serves 8

Working time: about 30 minutes

Total time: about 5 hours (includes marinating)

Calories 60
Protein 2g
Cholesterol 0mg
Total fat 4g
Saturated fat 1g
Sodium 60mg

15 cl	dry white wine	**¼ pint**
1	lemon, juice only	**1**
1	garlic clove, crushed	**1**
250 g	oyster mushrooms, trimmed, wiped and sliced	**8 oz**
250 g	button mushrooms, trimmed and wiped	**8 oz**
175 g	fresh shiitake mushrooms,	**6 oz**
2 tbsp	virgin olive oil	**2 tbsp**
2 tbsp	chopped parsley	**2 tbsp**
¼ tsp	salt	**¼ tsp**
	freshly ground black pepper	
	oakleaf or other lettuce leaves washed and dried	

In a large saucepan, combine the wine, lemon juice and garlic and bring the mixture to the boil. Add the prepared mushrooms, reduce the heat, cover the pan and cook gently until the mushrooms are tender but not overcooked—6 to 8 minutes.

Place a colander over a bowl and drain the mushrooms, reserving the liquid. Return the mushroom juices to the saucepan, bring to the boil and reduce to 15 cl (¼ pint). Remove the pan from the heat and whisk in the oil, parsley, salt and some pepper. Pour this mixture into a bowl and add the drained mushrooms. Let the mushrooms cool in the marinade, then cover the bowl with plastic film and refrigerate for at least 4 hours, or overnight.

Arrange the lettuce leaves on eight plates. Using a slotted spoon, lift the mushrooms from the marinade and transfer them to the plates. Spoon a little of the marinade over them and serve them immediately.

Editor's Note: Any combination of cultivated or edible wild mushrooms can be used in this marinade.

Sole and Cucumber Croustades

Serves 4

Working
(and total)
time: about
25 minutes

Calories
140
Protein
8g
Cholesterol
15mg
Total fat
4g
Saturated fat
2g
Sodium
180mg

4	slices white bread	4	100 g	fromage frais	3½ oz
15 g	unsalted butter, melted	½ oz	1 tbsp	coarsely chopped fresh dill	1 tbsp
4 tsp	dry vermouth	4 tsp		white pepper	
35 cl	unsalted fish stock	12 fl oz	5 cm	piece cucumber, halved	2 inch
175 g	sole fillets, skinned and cut into 2.5 cm (1 inch) cubes	6 oz		lengthwise, seeded, each half cut into eight thin wedges	

Preheat the oven to 190°C (375°F or Mark 5). Trim the bread into rounds about 10 cm (4 inches) in diameter. Lightly grease four 7.5 cm (3 inch) tartlet moulds, press the bread slices into the containers, top with squares of greaseproof paper and weight them down with baking beans. Bake the cases for 5 minutes, to set their shape. Remove the baking beans and carefully lift the baked bread cases out of their moulds with the tip of a blunt knife.

Brush the bread cases lightly with the butter on all sides, put them back in their moulds and return to the oven until golden-brown—about 15 minutes.

Meanwhile, prepare the filling. In a small saucepan, boil the vermouth until it is almost completely evaporated. Stir in the stock and heat the mixture until it barely simmers. Add the sole pieces and poach for 15 seconds. Using a slotted spoon, lift out the fish, drain it on absorbent paper towels, and keep it warm while you complete the sauce.

Return the stock to the boil and cook until reduced to about 2 tablespoons. Reduce the heat to very low and stir in the *fromage frais*. Heat the sauce through, stirring, but do not allow boil. Add the dill and a little white pepper.

Gently stir the fish strips and cucumber pieces into the sauce. Remove the bread cases from the oven, spoon the filling into them and serve hot.

9

Spirals with Lemon Sauce and Dill

<table>
<tr><td>Serves 4

Working
(and total)
time: about
20 minutes</td><td></td><td>Calories
290
Protein
9g
Cholesterol
10mg
Total fat
3g
Saturated fat
1g
Sodium
100mg</td></tr>
</table>

250 g	spirals	**8 oz**	
¼ litre	milk	**8 fl oz**	
½ tsp	salt	**½ tsp**	
4 tbsp	aquavit, or 4 tbsp vodka and 1 tsp caraway seeds	**4 tbsp**	

3 tbsp	fresh lemon juice	**3 tbsp**
5 cm	strip of lemon rind	**2 inch**
2 tbsp	finely cut fresh dill, or 2 tsp dried dill	**2 tbsp**

Put the milk, salt, aquavit or vodka and caraway seeds, lemon juice and lemon rind in a large non-stick or heavy frying pan. Bring the liquid to the boil, reduce the heat and simmer gently for 3 minutes. Add the spirals and enough water to almost cover them. Cover the pan and cook over low heat, removing the lid and stirring occasionally, until the spirals are *al dente* and about 4 tablespoons of sauce remains—approximately 15 minutes. (If necessary, add more water to keep the spirals from sticking.) Remove the lemon rind and discard it. Stir in the chopped dill and serve the dish immediately.

Tossed Salad with Eggs and French Beans

Serves 6

Working time: about 15 minutes

Total time: about 40 minutes (includes marinating)

Calories 115
Protein 3g
Cholesterol 75mg
Total fat 10g
Saturated fat 2g
Sodium 100mg

½	small red onion, cut thinly into rings	½
1	small red lollo lettuce, washed and dried, leaves torn	1
30 g	rocket, washed and dried	1 oz
90 g	French beans, topped and blanched for 3 minutes in boiling water	3 oz
2	eggs, hard-boiled, each cut into six wedges	2

6	black olives	6
3	red basil sprigs	3
3	green basil sprigs	3
	Vinaigrette dressing	
1	garlic clove, crushed	1
¼ tsp	salt	¼ tsp
	freshly ground black pepper	
1 tbsp	red wine vinegar	1 tbsp
3 tbsp	virgin olive oil	3 tbsp

First prepare the vinaigrette. Place the garlic, salt and some pepper in a large salad bowl. Using a wooden pestle, pound the ingredients until they break down into a paste. Add the vinegar and stir until the salt dissolves. Pour in the olive oil and mix thoroughly.

With your hands or the pestle, stir the onion slices into the vinaigrette to coat them well. Set them aside to marinate for 30 minutes.

Cross a pair of salad servers over the bottom of the bowl, to keep the dressing separate from the leaves that will be added before the salad is tossed. Lay a few of the largest lettuce leaves on the servers, then fill the bowl with the remaining lettuce and the rocket.

Top the leaves with the French beans, hard-boiled eggs, olives and basil. Draw out the servers from the bed of lettuce and rocket and toss the salad with the servers, or by hand, until all its ingredients are lightly coated with the dressing.

Artichoke and Potato Bowl

Serves 4

Working time:
about 20
minutes

Total time:
about 1 hour
and 20 minutes
(includes
chilling)

Calories
150
Protein
2g
Cholesterol
0mg
Total fat
10g
Saturated fat
2g
Sodium
35mg

2 tbsp	fresh lemon juice or vinegar	**2 tbsp**
350 g	baby artichokes, stems removed outer leaves removed	**12 oz**
250 g	small new potatoes, scrubbed	**8 oz**
1	small head radicchio	**1**
1	small head lettuce,	**1**
2 tbsp	finely cut chives	**2 tbsp**

Balsamic vinaigrette

1 tbsp	balsamic vinegar	**1 tbsp**
¼ tsp	dry mustard	**¼ tsp**
½	garlic clove, finely chopped	**½**
	freshly ground black pepper	
2½ tbsp	virgin olive oil	**2½ tbsp**

Add lemon juice or vinegar to a large saucepan of boiling water. Submerge the artichokes by weighting them down with a heavy plate or the lid from a smaller saucepan, and cook until tender—20 to 25 minutes. Drain them and set aside to cool. Meanwhile, cut the potatoes in half and cook them in a covered pan of boiling water until tender—about 12 minutes.

To make the vinaigrette, place the balsamic vinegar in a small jar with a lid and add the mustard, garlic and some pepper. Stir the ingredients to combine them, then add the oil. Cover and shake it to mix everything well. When the potatoes are cooked, transfer

them to a large bowl. Shake the jar of dressing again and add some of this while the potatoes are hot. Toss the potatoes.

Cut off the top 2.5 cm (1 inch) of the cooked artichokes and remove any leaves that are still fibrous. Cut the artichokes in half lengthwise and remove the fuzzy choke if there is one. Add the halves to the potatoes. Shake the jar of dressing again and add the remaining dressing to the salad. Toss the vegetables. Cover the salad with plastic film and chill in the refrigerator for about 30 minutes.

Line a large salad bowl with the radicchio and lettuce, scatter the salad and sprinkle it with chopped chives before serving.

Parsley and Burghul Salad

Serves 6

Working time:
about 10
minutes

Total time:
about 1 hour
(includes
soaking and
cooling)

Calories
155
Protein
4g
Cholesterol
0mg
Total fat
8g
Saturated fat
1g
Sodium
75mg

125 g	burghul	4 oz
125 g	parsley leaves, chopped	4 oz
60 g	fresh mint leaves, chopped	2 oz
4	spring onions, chopped	4
4 tbsp	fresh lemon juice	4 tbsp

3 tbsp	virgin olive oil	3 tbsp
¼ tsp	salt	¼ tsp
	freshly ground black pepper	
1	tomato, cut into thin wedges	1

Place the burghul in a bowl, cover it with 60 cl (1 pint) of boiling water, and leave it to soak for 30 minutes. Drain the soaked burghul through a colander lined with muslin and squeeze it dry, a handful at a time, extracting as much water as possible.

Place the burghul in a mixing bowl. Add the parsley, mint, spring onions, lemon juice, oil, salt and some pepper. Mix the ingredients thoroughly, and leave the salad in a cool place for 15 to 20 minutes to allow its flavours to blend.

Turn the salad out on to a shallow dish or platter and serve it garnished with the tomato wedges.

Mediterranean Vegetable Stew

Serves 6

Working time: about 35 minutes

Total time: about 2 hours and 45 minutes (includes cooling)

Calories 45
Protein 2g
Cholesterol 0mg
Total fat 3g
Saturated fat 1g
Sodium 175mg

2	large tomatoes, skinned, seeded and chopped	2
6	baby artichokes, halved	6
2 tbsp	fresh lemon juice	2 tbsp
4	sticks celery, sliced	4
1	fennel bulb, thinly sliced	1
3	thin leeks, trimmed and sliced into 1 cm (½ inch) rings	3
1	bayleaf	1
12	pearl onions	12
1 tbsp	virgin olive oil	1 tbsp
300 g	chestnut or button mushrooms, wiped clean, stalks trimmed,	10 oz
½ tsp	salt	½ tsp
	freshly ground black pepper	
1 tbsp	chopped fennel leaves	1 tbsp

In a large, heavy-bottomed saucepan, heat the tomatoes, artichokes and lemon juice, stirring frequently until the mixture comes to the boil. Continue to cook the vegetables over high heat, stirring occasionally, for another 10 minutes.

Add the celery, fennel, leeks and bay leaf to the tomatoes and artichokes, and simmer uncovered, stirring occasionally, until the vegetables are almost tender—about 20 minutes.

Meanwhile, in a small, heavy-bottomed saucepan, sauté the onions in the oil until they are soft and well browned—about 20 minutes. Shake the saucepan frequently to prevent the onions from sticking to the bottom or burning.

When the vegetables in the large pan are nearly cooked, add the mushrooms and simmer for another 10 minutes. Remove the pan from the heat and mix in the salt, some pepper and the onions. Leave the mixture to cool for about 2 hours.

Remove the bay leaf and discard it. Before serving, transfer the stew to a large serving dish and sprinkle the fennel leaves over the top.

Aubergines in Tomato Sauce

Serves 6

Working time:
about 20
minutes

Total time:
about 2 hours

Calories
100
Protein
3g
Cholesterol
0mg
Total fat
6g
Saturated fat
1g
Sodium
75mg

500 g	aubergines, sliced	1 lb
1¼ tsp	salt	1¼ tsp
2 tbsp	virgin olive oil	2 tbsp
750 g	ripe tomatoes, skinned, seeded and chopped, or 400 g (14 oz) canned tomatoes, drained and coarsely chopped	1½ lb
1	onion, sliced	1

2	garlic cloves, chopped	2
1 tsp	tomato paste	1 tsp
1	bay leaf	1
	freshly ground black pepper	
15 g	pine-nuts, tossed in a heavy frying pan over medium heat until golden-brown	½ oz
1 tbsp	chopped parsley	1 tbsp

Sprinkle the aubergine slices with 1 teaspoon of the salt and let them drain in a colander for 30 minutes to draw out their bitter juices. Meanwhile, heat the oil in a large, heavy-bottomed saucepan, and fry the sliced onion and the garlic until they are softened. Add the chopped tomatoes, tomato paste, bay leaf, the remaining salt and some pepper, then cover the pan and simmer the sauce for 10 minutes.

Rinse the aubergines in cold water and pat them dry with kitchen paper. Add the aubergines to the pan, coat them with the sauce, then cover the saucepan and simmer the mixture gently for a further 30 minutes. Remove the bay leaf.

Let the sauced aubergines cool in the pan. Turn them out on to a shallow dish, sprinkle them with the pine-nuts and parsley, and serve at room temperature.

Macerated Mackerel

Serves 6

Working time:
about 20
minutes

Total time: 1
to 2 days
(includes
marinating)

Calories
210
Protein
16g
Cholesterol
40mg
Total fat
7g
Saturated fat
3g
Sodium
370mg

4	mackerel, cleaned, skinned, filleted	4
1 tsp	salt	1 tsp
½ tsp	caster sugar	½ tsp
1 tsp	coriander seeds, finely crushed	1 tsp
2 tsp	fresh lime or lemon juice	2 tsp
4 tbsp	apple juice	4 tbsp
1	red apple	1
4	red lollo lettuce leaves	4

4	small radicchio leaves,	4
2 tbsp	coriander leaves	2 tbsp
2 tsp	sesame seeds	2 tsp
	Apple dressing	
3 tbsp	apple juice	3 tbsp
1 tsp	virgin olive oil	1 tsp
½ tsp	fresh lime or lemon juice	½ tsp
	white pepper	

Place two fillets in a shallow dish. Pound the salt, sugar and coriander seeds together. Spread half over the fillets. Mix the lime or lemon juice with the apple juice and sprinkle 3 tablespoons of this over the fish.

Lay on the remaining fillets and spread on the rest of the salt, sugar and spice mixture. Spoon on the remaining juices. Cover with plastic film, set a weighted board on top, and leave in a cool place (not refrigerator) to marinate for one to two days. An hour before serving put six plates in the refrigerator. Cut the fillets diagonally into thin slices.

For the dressing, place the apple juice and oil in a small bowl and whisk well. Stir in the lime or lemon juice and some white pepper.

Divide the mackerel slices among the plates, arranging in a semi-circle. Core and thinly slice the apple. Tear the red lollo lettuce and radicchio leaves, and toss them lightly in half of the dressing together with the apple slices, coriander leaves. Scatter the salad on the serving plates alongside the fish. Spoon the remaining dressing over the mackerel, sprinkle the fish with the sesame seeds and serve.

Sweet-and-Sour Herring

Serves 8

Working time:
about 20
minutes

Total time:
about 6 hours
(includes
marinating)

Calories
150
Protein
12g
Cholesterol
25mg
Total fat
6g
Saturated fat
1g
Sodium
40mg

¼ litre	white wine vinegar	8 fl oz
2.5 cm	piece fresh ginger root, bruised with a pestle or a heavy knife, plus ½ tsp grated fresh ginger root	1 inch
2	bay leaves	2
1	lime, rind only	1
1 tbsp	sugar	1 tbsp

¼ tsp	allspice berries	¼ tsp
½ tsp	white pepper	½ tsp
5	herrings, boned and cut into 2.5 cm (1 inch) slices	5
375 g	fromage frais	13 oz
3	spring onions, chopped	3
1 tbsp	chopped chives	1 tbsp
1	red onion, cut into rings	1

In a large saucepan, bring the wine vinegar and ¼ litre (8 fl oz) of water to the boil with the piece of ginger root, the bay leaves, lime rind, sugar, all spice berries and white pepper. Simmer the mixture for 5 minutes, then set it aside to cool. Place the fillets in a shallow non-reactive bowl, cover them with the spiced vinegar mixture, and marinate them in the refrigerator for 4 to 6 hours.

Remove the fillets from the marinade and wipe them dry with paper towels. In a mixing bowl, combine the fromage frais, grated ginger root, spring onions and chopped chives. Toss the fish in this mixture until it is thoroughly coated. Transfer the sauced herrings to a serving dish, garnish them with the red onion rings and serve immediately.

Italian Seafood Salad

Serves 8

Working time:
about 1 hour

Total time:
about 4 hours
(includes
marinating)

Calories
120
Protein
14g
Cholesterol
100mg
Total fat
6g
Saturated fat
1g
Sodium
155mg

1½ tbsp	virgin olive oil	1½ tbsp
1	onion, chopped	1
500 g	squid, cleaned and rinsed thoroughly, pouches cut into rings, wings sliced into strips, tentacles left whole	1 lb
1	garlic clove, crushed	1
1 tbsp	fresh lemon juice	1 tbsp
1 tbsp	chopped parsley	1 tbsp

¼ tsp	salt	¼ tsp
	freshly ground black pepper	
175 g	peeled prawns, halved lengthwise and deveined	6 oz
3	sticks celery, thinly sliced	3
250 g	round or other lettuce, washed, dried and shredded	8 oz
1	red onion, thinly sliced	1
2	lemons, cut into wedges	2

In a saucepan, heat ½ tablespoon of the oil, add the onion and cook it gently until it is softened, but not browned—6 to 8 minutes. Add the prepared squid and the garlic, cover the saucepan and cook gently until the squid is very tender—15 to 20 minutes. Drain the squid in a colander set over a bowl, and return the squid juices to the saucepan; boil the liquid over high heat until it is reduced by three quarters. Whisk the remaining oil, the lemon juice, parsley, salt and some freshly ground black pepper into the squid juices to make a marinade.

Put the cooked squid and the prawns into a bowl, pour the marinade over them and mix the seafood until it is well coated. Cover the mixture and place it in the refrigerator to marinate for at least 3 hours.

Before serving, mix the sliced celery into the seafood. Serve the salad on a bed of shredded lettuce garnished with a few red onion rings, and accompanied by the lemon wedges.

Editor's Note: If you are using baby squid they will cook more rapidly. Test them for tenderness after cooking for about 5 minutes.

Sole and Asparagus Tartlets

Serves 6

Working time:
about 1 hour

Total time:
about 3 hours
(includes
chilling)

Calories
240
Protein
12g
Cholesterol
50mg
Total fat
13g
Saturated fat
3g
Sodium
260mg

175 g	skinned sole fillets	**6 oz**
1	egg white	**1**
2 tbsp	thick Greek yogurt	**2 tbsp**
¼ tsp	salt	**¼ tsp**
	freshly ground black pepper	
250 g	asparagus, thinly sliced	**8 oz**
45 g	smoked salmon, cut in strips	**1½ oz**

2 tsp	finely cut chives	**2 tsp**
	thinly sliced cucumber, for garnish	
	Tartlet shells	
125 g	plain flour	**4 oz**
¼ tsp	salt	**¼ tsp**
60 g	polyunsaturated margarine	**2 oz**
1	egg yolk	**1**

Blend the fillets and egg white in a food processor until they form a smooth paste, then work through a sieve to remove coarse fibres. Cover and refrigerate.

For the pastry, sift the flour and salt into a bowl and rub in the margarine until the mixture resembles fine breadcrumbs. Make a well and pour in the egg yolk and 1 tablespoon of water. Mix until dough is formed. Knead the dough and roll out thinly. Cut out rounds to line 6 fluted tartlet tins. Prick the pastry and refrigerate for 30 minutes. Preheat the oven to 220°C (425°F or Mark 7).

Remove the sole from the refrigerator and beat in half of the yogurt, the salt and some pepper. Cover and return to refrigerator.

Cook the sliced asparagus in boiling water until tender—1 to 2 minutes. Refresh and drain.

Bake the pastry shells for 10 minutes. Remove from the oven and reduce the temperature to 180°C (350°F or Mark 4). Divide the asparagus equally among the pastry cases. Spoon the sole mixture on top, spreading evenly. Return tartlets to oven and cook until the mixture is lightly set—6 to 8 minutes.

Remove tartlets from the oven, let cool, cover with foil and refrigerate for two hours. Spread the remaining yogurt in a thin layer over the top of each tartlet, arrange strips of salmon around its edges, and garnish with the cucumber and chives.

Okra Stuffed with Indian Spices

Serves 4

Working (and total) time: about 40 minutes

Calories
60
Protein
6g
Cholesterol
10mg
Total fat
2g
Saturated fat
1g
Sodium
125mg

20	okra	20
1 tsp	coriander seeds	1 tsp
½ tsp	yellow mustard seeds	½ tsp
4	garlic cloves	4
¼ tsp	turmeric	¼ tsp
½ tsp	freshly ground black pepper	½ tsp
1 tbsp	finely cut chives plus four whole chives	1 tbsp
2½ tbsp	cottage cheese	2½ tbsp
	Coriander-yogurt sauce	
½ tbsp	yellow mustard seeds	½ tbsp
6 tbsp	thick Greek yogurt	6 tbsp
½ tbsp	chopped fresh coriander leaves	½ tbsp
¼ tsp	white pepper	¼ tsp
½	garlic clove, crushed	½
1 tsp	fresh lemon juice	1 tsp

For the sauce, toast the mustard seeds in a heavy frying pan over medium heat for a few seconds until they begin to pop, then crush them in a mortar. Stir together the yogurt, coriander leaves, crushed mustard seeds, pepper, garlic and the lemon juice. Set aside.

With a sharp knife, make a slit along the length of each okra pod, being careful not to split the ends, and remove the seeds.

Toast the coriander and mustard seeds in a heavy frying pan over medium heat for a few seconds until the seeds pop and begin to release their aroma. Place the seeds in a mortar with the garlic, turmeric and black

pepper and pound them to a paste. Stir in the finely cut chives and cottage cheese and continue until everything is blended.

Stuff each pod with some of the paste, pressing the edges of the slit together so the stuffing will not leak out as it cooks. Tie five of the pods together in a bundle with a long piece of chive. Repeat the process to form four bundles. Tuck the loose ends of the chives neatly underneath the okra parcels and place them in a steamer. Steam over boiling water until tender and bright green—about 5 minutes.

Serve the okra bundles on individual plates with the coriander-yogurt sauce.

Mint-Stuffed Courgettes with Tomato Coulis

Serves 6

Working time:
about 30
minutes

Total time:
about 50
minutes

Calories
55
Protein
5g
Cholesterol
5mg
Total fat
2g
Saturated fat
1g
Sodium
180mg

6	small courgettes, halved lengthwise	**6**
45 g	fresh mint, leaves only	**1½ oz**
125 g	low-fat curd cheese	**4 oz**
2 tbsp	breadcrumbs	**2 tbsp**
¼ tsp	salt	**¼ tsp**
	freshly ground black pepper	
2	egg whites	**2**

	Tomato coulis	
500 g	fresh tomatoes, skinned, seeded and chopped, or 400 g (14 oz) canned plum tomatoes	**1 lb**
1	garlic clove, chopped	**1**
1 tsp	chili powder	**1 tsp**
15 g	unsalted butter	**½ oz**
¼ tsp	salt	**¼ tsp**

Cook the courgette halves in salted boiling water until they are just tender—about 5 minutes. Drain, rinse, and leave them to cool on paper towels.

Preheat the oven to 200°C (400°F or Mark 6). When the courgettes are cool enough to handle, scoop out their centres with a teaspoon and transfer the flesh to a food processor or blender. Add the mint leaves and purée the mixture. Place the purée in a large bowl and add the curd cheese, breadcrumbs, salt and plenty of black pepper. In another bowl, beat the egg whites until they are stiff; fold them into the stuffing.

Arrange the courgette halves on a greased baking sheet and fill their centres with stuffing. Bake for about 25 minutes, until the stuffing acquires a golden tinge.

Meanwhile, bring the tomatoes to the boil in a heavy-bottomed saucepan. Add the garlic and the chili powder, and simmer the mixture for 15 minutes. Put the tomatoes into the food processor with the butter and the salt, and blend until the tomatoes break down to a purée and the butter is thoroughly incorporated. If you are using canned tomatoes, pass the sauce through a sieve. Return the sauce to the pan and cook over gentle heat until it is heated through—about 5 minutes. Serve the courgettes hot, accompanied by the tomato coulis.

Asparagus Soufflés

Serves 6

Working time:
about 45
minutes

Total time:
about 1 hour

Calories
75
Protein
5g
Cholesterol
20mg
Total fat
6g
Saturated fat
3g
Sodium
30mg

350 g	medium asparagus, trimmed and peeled to about 2.5 cm (1 inch) below the tips	**12 oz**	
30 g	unsalted butter	**1 oz**	
30 g	plain flour	**1 oz**	

125 g	low-fat ricotta cheese	**4 oz**	
¾ tsp	Dijon mustard	**¾ tsp**	
¼ tsp	freshly grated nutmeg	**¼ tsp**	
	freshly ground black pepper		
4	egg whites	**4**	

Preheat the oven to 190°C (375°F or Mark 5).

Cut off six of the asparagus tips, reserving the stalks. Bring a large saucepan of water to the boil, add the six tips and simmer until just tender—about 4 minutes. Refresh and set aside. Add the reserved stalks and remaining whole spears to the pan and simmer until very tender—about 15 minutes.

While the asparagus is cooking, butter six 12.5 cl (4 fl oz) ramekin dishes. Drain the stalks and blend them in a food processor until smooth. Rub the purée through a sieve placed over a bowl; discard the pulp left in the sieve.

Melt the butter in a saucepan. When it bubbles, add the flour and stir until the butter has been incorporated. Whisk in the asparagus purée, which will be thin. Continue whisking over low heat until the mixture is thick and bubbling. While the sauce cools, push the ricotta cheese through a sieve. Add the ricotta cheese to the sauce with the mustard, nutmeg and some pepper, and stir until smooth.

Beat the egg whites until beginning to form peaks. Add a large spoonful of the whites to the purée and whisk in to lighten the mixture, then use a metal spoon to fold in the remaining whites, until evenly blended. Spoon the mixture into the prepared ramekins.

Insert one reserved asparagus tip into the centre of each ramekin, making sure it just clears the surface of the mixture. Arrange the ramekins on a baking sheet and bake the soufflés until they are puffed up and tinged golden-brown, with their centres still soft and not firmly set—15 to 20 minutes. Serve hot.

Gingered Crab Meat Crêpes

Serves 8

Working
(and total)
time: about
45 minutes

Calories
140
Protein
9g
Cholesterol
75mg
Total fat
8g
Saturated fat
2g
Sodium
195mg

60 g	plain flour	**2 oz**
⅛ tsp	salt	**⅛ tsp**
1	egg	**1**
15cl	skimmed milk	**¼ pint**
15g	unsalted butter, melted	**½ oz**
8	small spring onions (optional)	**8**
1 tsp	safflower oil	**1 tsp**

Gingered crab meat filling

15 g	unsalted butter	**½ oz**
1	onion, very finely chopped	**1**
5 cm	piece ginger root, chopped	**2 inch**
20cm	cucumber, cut into sticks	**8 inch**
250 g	fresh crab meat, picked over	**8 oz**
8 cl	single cream	**3 fl oz**
	freshly ground black pepper	

To make the crêpe batter, sift the flour and salt into a bowl and make a well in the centre. Break the egg into the well and whisk. As the mixture thickens, whisk in the milk. Continue to slowly add the milk until it is all incorporated into the batter. Whisk in the melted butter, then cover the bowl and set aside for about 30 minutes.

Meanwhile, trim the spring onions, discarding the green tops and the root tips. To fashion onion brushes, make four short cuts at each end of the onion, turning after each cut and being careful to leave the mid-section intact. Place the onions in a bowl of iced water and leave in the refrigerator for about 30 minutes.

To prepare the crab meat filling, melt the butter in a frying pan, add the finely chopped onion and cook gently until it is softened but not browned—5 to 6 minutes. Add the ginger and the cucumber sticks and continue cooking for about 5 minutes. Stir in the crab meat and the cream and season with black pepper.

Heat the oil in a small frying pan and make eight crêpes. Stack and keep warm.

Set the crab filling over medium heat and stir until it is thoroughly heated through. Spoon an eighth of the crab filling on to one half of a crêpe, fold over to enclose the filling, then fold again. Serve immediately, garnished with the spring onion brushes.

Mussels in White Wine

Serves 8

Working
(and total)
time about
30 minutes

Calories
120
Protein
13g
Cholesterol
30mg
Total fat
5g
Saturated fat
3g
Sodium
195mg

2 kg	mussels, scrubbed and debearded	4 lb
1	onion, chopped	1
3	garlic cloves, crushed	3
2	bay leaves	2
60 g	parsley, finely chopped	2 oz

3	thyme sprigs	3
30 g	unsalted butter	1 oz
	freshly ground black pepper	
¼ litre	white wine	8 fl oz

Place the mussels in a large saucepan with the onions, garlic, bay leaves, parsley and thyme. Add the butter and some pepper, and pour in the wine. Cover and cook over high heat, lifting and shaking the pan several times, until the shells have opened—3 to 5 minutes, depending on the size and number of mussels.

With a slotted spoon, transfer the mussels to individual soup plates, discarding the bay leaves and any mussels that remain closed. Pour the cooking liquid through a strainer into the soup plates, and serve the mussels hot in their broth.

Steamed Clams with Spinach

Serves 4

Working (and total) time: about 20 minutes

Calories
115
Protein
9g
Cholesterol
20mg
Total fat
4g
Saturated fat
2g
Sodium
100mg

1 tbsp	unsalted butter	1 tbsp
1	onion, finely chopped	1
1	garlic clove, finely chopped	1
12.5 cl	white wine	4 fl oz
1 tbsp	chopped parsley	1 tbsp

¼ tsp	freshly ground black pepper	¼ tsp
750 g	small clams in their shells	1½ lb
250 g	fresh spinach, washed, stems removed, leaves shredded	8 oz
1	lemon, quartered	1

Melt the butter in a deep, non-reactive saucepan, add the onion and garlic, and cook, stirring continuously, until the onion is soft but not coloured—about 5 minutes. Stir in the wine, parsley and pepper, and bring the mixture to the boil. Add the clams and cook them for 5 minutes, covered, until their shells begin to open. With a slotted spoon, remove the clams from the pan and discard the loose top half of each shell. Place the clams in a warmed dish and cover with a tea towel.

Simmer the spinach in the wine and onion mixture for 2 minutes over moderate heat. When the spinach is cooked, drain it thoroughly in a colander set over a bowl. Press the spinach to drain off any excess liquid. Return the liquid to the pan. Divide the spinach among four plates, and place an equal number of clams on top of each portion.

Bring the reserved pan juices to the boil and cook over high heat for 1 minute to reduce them. Spoon the juices over the clams and spinach, and serve them garnished with the lemon wedges.

Editor's Note: Cockles may be substituted for the clams.

Sardines in Vine Leaves

Serves 4

Working time:
about 15
minutes

Total time:
about 1 hour
and15 minutes
(includes
marinating)

Calories
140
Protein
8g
Cholesterol
30mg
Total fat
11g
Saturated fat
2g
Sodium
225mg

8	small sardine, gutted (about 125g/4 oz each)	**8**	**8**	fresh thyme sprigs, or 1 tsp dried thyme	**8**
2 tbsp	virgin olive oil	**2 tbsp**	**8**	fresh oregano sprigs, or 1 tsp dried oregano	**8**
1	lemon, juice only	**1**	**8**	fresh vine leaves, or preserved vine leaves rinsed	**8**
1	garlic clove, finely chopped	**1**			
¼ tsp	salt	**¼ tsp**			

Rinse the sardines and pat them dry. In a dish large enough to hold all the fish in a single layer, mix together the olive oil, lemon juice, chopped garlic and salt. Place the fish in the dish, turning them in the marinade. Cover the dish with a lid or plastic film and place in the refrigerator for 1 hour. Turn the sardines once while they are marinating.

Preheat the grill. Remove the fish from the marinade and place each one on a vine leaf, together with a sprig of thyme and a sprig of oregano, or a sprinkling of dried thyme and oregano. Roll up the sardines in the vine leaves, tuck the ends of the leaves underneath the fish to form secure parcels and place them on the grill rack.

Grill the sardines for 3 minutes on each side, watching carefully to make sure the parcels do not burn. Place two of the wrapped sardines on each plate and serve the fish immediately, to be unwrapped at the table. When the leaves are pulled off, the fish skins and scales will come away with them.

Editor's Note: The technique described for grilling sardines can also be used with small red mullet.

Salmon Tartare

Serves 4

Working time:
about 20
minutes

Total time:
about 1 hour
and 20 minutes
(includes
chilling)

Calories
200
Protein
12g
Cholesterol
35mg
Total fat
9g
Saturated fat
1g
Sodium
195mg

250 g	salmon fillet, skinned and finely chopped	**8 oz**
½ tsp	freshly ground black pepper	**½ tsp**
2	spring onions, finely sliced	**2**

1	lime, finely grated rind only	**1**
6 tbsp	soured cream	**6 tbsp**
4	slices wholemeal bread, toasted, crusts removed	**4**

In a bowl, mix the chopped fish thoroughly with the black pepper and combine it with the spring onions. Chill the salmon mixture in the refrigerator for 1 hour.

In the meantime, stir most of the grated lime rind into the soured cream. Place the soured cream mixture and four individual serving plates in the refrigerator to chill with the salmon.

At serving time, divide the salmon tartare among the four chilled plates, forming each portion into a small mound with a hollow in its centre. Spoon a quarter of the soured cream mixture into each hollow and sprinkle on the remaining lime rind. Serve the fish accompanied by the wholemeal toast.

Editor's Note: Because the salmon in this recipe is not cooked, only the freshest fish should be used.

Sea Trout and Sweetcorn Papillotes

Serves 6

Working (and total) time: about 35 minutes

Calories 150
Protein 8g
Cholesterol 35mg
Total fat 9g
Saturated fat 1g
Sodium 290mg

30	baby sweetcorn cobs	30
2¼ tbsp	sesame oil	2¼ tbsp
2.5 cm	fresh ginger root, grated	1 inch
60 g	chives, finely cut	2 oz
350 g	sea trout fillet, boned, skinned and cut into six pieces	10 oz

¼ tbsp	salt	¼ tbsp
60 g	chives, finely cut	2 oz
	mixed green, pink, white and black peppercorns, coarsely ground	
2 tbsp	fresh lemon juice	2 tbsp

Preheat the oven to 240°C (475°F or Mark 9).

In a saucepan, bring 60 cl (1 pint) of lightly salted water to the boil, add the baby sweetcorn cobs and cook them until they are tender—about 5 minutes. Drain the cobs in a colander, and set aside to cool.

Meanwhile, cut out six 20 cm (8 inch) squares of greaseproof paper, and grease the centre of each square with a little sesame oil, leaving an ungreased outer rim of about 4 cm (1½ inches) on all sides.

Put four baby sweetcorns in the centre of each square and sprinkle the ginger over them. Place the chives on a flat plate and roll the fish in the chives until well coated. Top each pile of sweetcorn and ginger with a piece of fish, then set a final sweetcorn on top of the fish. Season each papillote assemblage with a little of the salt, a generous grinding of mixed peppercorns, and 1 teaspoon each of the sesame oil and lemon juice. Bring two opposite sides of the paper together and pleat them to enclose the fish. Make a 1 cm (½ inch) fold in each of the ends and fold over twice, pressing down firmly to seal the parcel. Repeat the process to make five more papillotes.

Place the parcels on a baking sheet, and bake them for 7 minutes. Serve them immediately, letting the· diners open their own papillotes at table to savour the aroma that emerges as the package is unwrapped.

Warm Skate Salad with Red Pepper Vinaigrette

Serves 6

Working (and total) time: about 45 minutes

Calories
95
Protein
8g
Cholesterol
25mg
Total fat
6g
Saturated fat
1g
Sodium
100mg

500 g	skate wings, skinned	1 lb
30 cl	white wine	½ pint
1	small onion, cut in half	1
1	garlic clove, unpeeled	1
1	small carrot peeled	1
1	parsley sprig	1
1	fresh thyme sprig	1
1	bayleaf	1

175 g	mange-tout, trimmed	6 oz
	Red pepper vinaigrette	
1 tbsp	red wine vinegar	1 tbsp
¼ tsp	salt	¼ tsp
2	sweet red peppers, skinned and sieved	2
	freshly ground black pepper	
2 tbsp	virgin olive oil	2 tbsp

Rinse the skinned skate wings well under cold running water. In a frying pan, combine the wine, 1 litre (1¾pints) of water, the onion, garlic, carrot, parsley, thyme and bay leaf. Bring to the boil, reduce the heat to medium low and add the skate. Poach the fish until the flesh is opaque and cooked through at the thickest part—about 15 minutes.

While the skate cooks, prepare the red pepper vinaigrette. In a small bowl, combine the wine vinegar with the salt, and stir until the salt dissolves. Stir in the sieved red pepper and some black pepper, then whisk in the oil until it is thoroughly blended.

Lift the poached skate wings from their cooking liquid with a slotted spoon, and transfer them to a plate. Blanch the mange-tout in rapidly boiling water for 30 seconds. Drain and refresh briefly under cold running water, then drain again. Arrange the mange-tout on six serving plates.

As soon as the fish is cool enough to handle, use your finger to lift the flesh, in strips, from the cartilage. Place a portion of skate on each bed of mange-tout. Stir the red pepper vinaigrette well with a fork, and serve it alongside the warm skate.

Smoked Haddock in Leek Wrappers

Serves 6
Working time:
about 35
minutes

Total time:
about 55
minutes

Calories
90
Protein
10g
Cholesterol
30mg
Total fat
4g
Saturated fat
2g
Sodium
450mg

3	large leeks, two outer most layers only, ends trimmed	**3**	**1 tbsp**	fresh lemon juice	**1 tbsp**
250 g	smoked haddock fillet	**8 oz**	**1**	shallot, finely chopped	**1**
1	egg	**1**	**15 g**	unsalted butter	**½ oz**
4 tbsp	plain low-fat yogurt	**4 tbsp**	**2 tsp**	finely cut chives	**2 tsp**
	freshly ground black pepper		**1 tsp**	finely chopped parsley	**1 tsp**
12.5 cl	dry white wine	**4 floz**	**⅛ tsp**	cayenne pepper	**⅛ tsp**
			½	lemon, thinly sliced	**½**

Bring a large saucepan of water to the boil, add the outer leek layers and blanch them for 2 minutes. Drain the layers, refresh them under cold water and dry them. Trim each layer to a rectangle 20 by 10 cm (8 by 4 inches), and set the wrappers aside.

Preheat the oven to 220°C (425°F or Mark 7). In a food processor, blend the smoked haddock fillet, egg, yogurt and pepper.

Lay out the leek wrappers on a flat surface. Place 2 teaspoons of the smoked haddock filling on the dark green end and roll up the packages, pressing them to seal in the filling.

Arrange the leek rolls seam side down in a shallow baking dish. Pour the wine and

lemon juice over the leeks and cover with dampened greaseproof paper. Bake the rolls until the filling is just set—15 to 20 minutes. Using a slotted spatula, transfer the leek rolls to a warmed platter and keep them hot.

Strain the juices from the baking dish into a small saucepan and add the shallot. Bring the liquid to the boil over high heat and boil it for 1 minute in order to reduce it slightly.

Remove the pan from the heat and stir in the butter, one piece at a time. Then spoon the sauce over the leek rolls. Add a sprinkling of chives and parsley, and a small pinch of cayenne, to each serving. Garnish with the lemon slices, and serve.

Squid in a Spanish Sauce

Serves 6
Working time:
about

25 minutes
Total time:
about 1 hour
and 10
minutes

Calories
135
Protein
14g
Cholesterol
100mg
Total fat
6g
Saturated fat
1g
Sodium
220mg

2 tbsp	virgin olive oil	2 tbsp
1	onion, halved and sliced thinly	1
750 g	small squid, cleaned, pouches cut into 1.5 cm (¾ inch) slices, small tentacles left whole, large tentacles sliced	1½ lb
2	garlic cloves, chopped	2
12.5 cl	red wine	4 fl oz
4	tomatoes, skinned, seeded and chopped	4
1 tbsp	tomato paste	1 tbsp
1	bay leaf	1
1	thyme sprig	1
¼ tsp	salt	¼ tsp
1 tbsp	chopped parsley	1 tbsp
	lemon wedges, for garnish	

Heat the oil in a heavy-bottomed saucepan and fry the onion until it is softened. Add the squid and the garlic and cook them for about 4 minutes, turning them occasionally, until the squid is firm and opaque.

Add the wine, tomatoes, tomato paste, bay leaf, thyme, salt and some pepper. Cover the pan and cook the squid until it is tender—about 45 minutes. Remove the bay leaf and the thyme sprig, then stir in the chopped parsley.

Turn the sauced squid into a serving dish and garnish with the lemon wedges.

Courgettes Filled with Crab

Serves 6

Working time:
about 30
minutes

Total time:
about 1 hour
and 10
minutes

Calories
80
Protein
2g
Cholesterol
35mg
Total fat
3g
Saturated fat
1g
Sodium
25mg

6	courgettes, about 125g (4 oz), trimmed and washed	**6**
15 g	unsalted butter	**½ oz**
1	very small onion, finely chopped	**1**
15 g	plain flour	**½ oz**
15 cl	dry white wine	**¼ pint**
175 g	fresh crab meat	**6 oz**
1 tbsp	single cream	**1 tbsp**
1 tsp	fresh lemon juice	**1 tsp**
¼ tsp	salt	**¼ tsp**
	freshly ground black pepper	
15 g	fresh white breadcrumbs	**½ oz**
1	small carrot, finely julienned	**1**

Preheat the oven to 190°C (375°F or Mark 5).

Cut the courgettes in half lengthwise and score the cut sides lightly with the tines of a fork or a sharp knife.

Grease a large, shallow ovenproof dish, and place the courgettes in the dish, cut side down. Cover them with aluminium foil and bake the courgettes until they are cooked through—45 to 50 minutes.

About 15 minutes before the courgettes are ready, melt the butter in a saucepan, then add the onion and cook it gently until it is very soft but not browned—3 to 4 minutes. Stir the flour into the onion and cook for 1 minute. Gradually stir the wine into the flour and

onion roux, then bring the mixture to the boil, stirring all the time until the sauce becomes very thick. Remove the saucepan from the heat, and stir in the crab meat, cream, lemon juice, salt and some pepper.

Preheat the grill.

When the courgettes are cooked, turn them over so the cut sides are uppermost. Divide the crab mixture evenly among the courgettes, spooning it neatly on top of the halves. Sprinkle the breadcrumbs evenly over the top and place the dish under the grill until the crab mixture is heated through and the breadcrumbs are golden-brown. Serve the courgettes hot, garnished with the carrot julienne.

Squab Salad with Wild Mushrooms

Serves 6

Working time:
about 35
minutes

Total time:
about 9 hours
(includes
marinating)

Calories
165
Protein
12g
Cholesterol
35mg
Total fat
12g
Saturated fat
2g
Sodium
70mg

4 tsp	balsamic vinegar	4 tsp
2 tsp	dry Madeira	2 tsp
4 tsp	walnut oil	4 tsp
½ tsp	Sichuan peppercorns, toasted and crushed (optional)	½ tsp
½ tsp	black peppercorns, coarsely ground	½ tsp
6	pigeon squab breasts, skinned	6

15 g	unsalted butter	½ oz
180 g	fresh wild mushrooms, such as chanterelles, ceps or shiitake	6 oz
⅛ tsp	salt	⅛ tsp
2 tsp	safflower oil	2 tsp
	freshly ground black pepper	
90 g	salad leaves, such as purslane or lamb's lettuce, washed and dried	3 oz

In a shallow bowl, combine 2 teaspoons of the balsamic vinegar, the Madeira, 2 teaspoons of the walnut oil and the two kinds of peppercorns. Place the pigeon breasts in the marinade and refrigerate them for at least 8 hours, turning them from time to time.

Shortly before serving, melt the butter in a saucepan and add the mushrooms. Toss with a wooden spoon until they begin to release their juices, then set aside.

Remove the pigeon breasts from the marinade without draining them, place them in a pan and sauté them over very high heat for 2 minutes on each side.

In a small bowl, stir the salt into the remaining balsamic vinegar, until it dissolves. Add the remaining walnut oil, the safflower oil and pepper and whisk the ingredients together until they are thoroughly blended.

Remove the pigeon breasts from the frying pan and slice each one into long, thin slices.

Pour the vinaigrette into the saucepan containing the wild mushrooms to warm through for a few seconds. Arrange the breasts, mushrooms and salad leaves on individual serving plates. Spoon the vinaigrette from the saucepan over the mushrooms. Serve the salad immediately.

Duck Brochettes with Spiced Wine Sauce

Serves 4

Working time: about 45 minutes

Total time: about 1 hour and 25 minutes (includes marinating)

Calories 210
Protein 18g
Cholesterol 70mg
Total fat 7g
Saturated fat 2g
Sodium 125 mg

350 g	boned duck breasts	**12 oz**
5 tbsp	red wine	**5 tbsp**
¼ tsp	salt	**¼ tsp**
1 tsp	mixed dried herbs, such as oregano, thyme and marjoram	**1 tsp**
½	small onion, finely chopped	**½**
125 g	oyster mushrooms, trimmed	**4 oz**
½ tsp	virgin olive oil	**4 oz**
	Red wine sauce	
1 tsp	grated orange rind	**1 tsp**
2 tbsp	fresh orange juice	**2 tbsp**
60 g	red currant jelly	**2 oz**
12.5 cl	red wine	**4 fl oz**
⅛ tsp	cayenne pepper	**⅛ tsp**

Carefully remove the skin and fat from the duck breasts. Cut the flesh into neat 2.5 cm (1 inch) cubes.

Put the red wine, salt, herbs and onion in a bowl and mix them well. Add the cubed duck flesh, turning the pieces in the marinade until they are evenly coated. Cover the bowl and allow the duck. to marinate at room temperature for at least 1 hour, turning the duck pieces occasionally.

Meanwhile, prepare the sauce. Combine the orange rind and juice, redcurrant jelly, wine and cayenne pepper in a small saucepan. Bring the mixture to the boil,

stirring constantly, then lower the heat and simmer the sauce gently until it is reduced by about half. Strain the sauce, return it to the pan, cover and keep warm over low heat while you grill the brochettes.

Preheat the grill to high. Remove the duck pieces from the marinade with a slotted spoon, and thread them alternately with the mushrooms on to small skewers. Place the brochettes on the grill rack and brush them with the oil. Grill the brochettes, turning them once, until the duck pieces are tender yet still slightly pink inside—4 to 5 minutes. Serve the brochettes hot, with the wine sauce on the side.

Miniature Meatballs

Serves 6

Working time:
about 40
minutes

Total time:
about 1 hour
and 30
minutes

Calories
220
Protein
21g
Cholesterol
75mg
Total fat
8g
Saturated fat
2g
Sodium
160mg

400 g	lean beef, minced	**14 oz**	**1**	onion, chopped		**1**
90 g	fresh wholemeal breadcrumbs	**3 oz**	**2**	garlic cloves, chopped		**2**
1 tbsp	chopped parsley	**1 tbsp**	**1**	small sweet red pepper, chopped		**1**
1	garlic clove, finely chopped	**1**	**250 g**	ripe tomatoes, skinned, seeded,		**8 oz**
1	egg	**1**		and chopped, or 200 g (7 oz)		
⅛ tsp	salt	**⅛ tsp**		canned tomatoes, drained		
	freshly ground black pepper			and chopped		
½ tbsp	virgin olive oil	**½ tbsp**	**⅛ tsp**	freshly ground black pepper		**⅛ tsp**
	Spanish sauce		**6 cl**	medium sherry		**2 fl oz**
1 tbsp	virgin olive oil	**1 tbsp**				

To make the sauce, heat the oil in a heavy, fireproof casserole and fry the onion and garlic until they are soft but not browned. Add the chopped red pepper, tomatoes, salt and some freshly ground black pepper, and simmer the mixture for 20 minutes. While it cooks, prepare the meatballs.

Preheat the oven to 180°C (350°F or Mark 4). Combine the beef, breadcrumbs, parsley, garlic, egg and 2 tablespoons of water in a large mixing bowl. Add the salt and some black pepper and mix the ingredients until

they are thoroughly blended. With dampened hands, shape the mixture into 36 miniature meatballs, each slightly smaller than a walnut.

Heat the oil in a heavy frying pan and fry the meatballs, turning them to prevent sticking, until they are browned. Remove them from the pan and drain them on paper towels.

Transfer the sauce to a blender or food processor, add the sherry, and purée the mixture. Return the sauce to the casserole, add the drained meatballs, and bake them for 40 minutes in the oven. Serve hot.

Crab and Paprika Soufflés

Serves 6

Working time: about 15 minutes

Total time: about 35 minutes

Calories 55
Protein 8g
Cholesterol 55mg
Total fat 2g
Saturated fat 1g
Sodium 150mg

175 g	cooked crab meat, picked over and chilled	6 oz	175 g	fromage frais	6 oz
1	egg yolk	1	2 tsp	paprika	2 tsp
½ tsp	fresh lemon juice	½ tsp	¼ tsp	salt	¼ tsp
			5	egg whites	5

Preheat the oven to 180°C (350°F or Mark 4).

In a large bowl, combine the chilled crab meat, egg yolk, lemon juice and *fomage frais*. Add the paprika and salt to the mixture.

Whisk the egg whites until they are stiff, but not dry, then fold them gently into the crab meat mixture. Divide the mixture among six 12.5 cl (4 fl oz) very lightly oiled ramekin dishes and place them in a baking tin. bake the soufflés until they are lightly set and golden-coloured—about 17 minutes—and serve immediately.

Spinach-Filled Cannelloni Gratins with Tomato Sauce

Serves 4

Working (and total) time: about 1 hour

Calories
165
Protein
10g
Cholesterol
15mg
Total fat
8g
Saturated fat
4g
Sodium
385mg

4	cannelloni tubes (about 90g/3oz)	4
750 g	spinach leaves, washed, stemmed, blanched in boiling water for 30 seconds, drained	1½ lb
15 g	unsalted butter	½ oz
1 tbsp	single cream	1 tbsp
¼ tsp	salt	¼ tsp
	freshly ground black pepper	
½ tsp	grated nutmeg	½ tsp
15 g	Parmesan cheese, grated	½ oz
15 g	dry wholemeal breadcrumbs	½ oz
1 tbsp	finely shredded basil leaves	1 tbsp

	Tomato sauce	
½ tbsp	virgin olive oil	½ tbsp
1	small onion, finely chopped	1
1	garlic clove, crushed	1
750 g	tomatoes, skinned, seeded and chopped, or 400 g (14 oz) canned tomatoes, drained and sieved	1½ lb
2 tbsp	finely shredded basil leaves	2 tbsp
¼ tsp	salt	¼ tsp
	freshly ground black pepper	

To make the tomato sauce, heat the oil in a heavy-bottomed saucepan, add the onion, and cook gently until the onion is softened but not browned. Stir in the garlic, tomatoes, basil, salt and some pepper. Cook the mixture, uncovered, until the sauce is thickened and reduced by half—about 30 minutes.

Meanwhile, cook the cannelloni tubes in a large pan of lightly salted boiling water until they are softened—3 to 4 minutes. Drain them, rinse, and allow them to drain once more.

For the filling, chop the spinach finely. Heat the butter in a small frying pan, add the spinach and heat through. Stir in the cream, the salt, pepper and the grated nutmeg. With a spoon, fill the tubes with the spinach mixture and place them in well-buttered dishes.

Spoon the sauce over the cannelloni, sprinkle generously with Parmesan cheese and breadcrumbs, and grill them until golden-brown—about 5 minutes. Sprinkle with the shredded basil and serve immediately.

Baked Oysters

Makes 12
oysters

Working time:
about 30
minutes

Total time:
about 40
minutes

Per oyster:
Calories
45
Protein
5g
Cholesterol
20mg
Total fat
2g
Saturated fat
1g
Sodium
190mg

350 g	spinach, washed and stemmed	**12 oz**
15 g	unsalted butter	**¼ oz**
6	spring onions, trimmed and finely sliced	**6**
	freshly ground black pepper	
12	fresh oysters	**12**

	coarse salt for baking	
	Parmesan topping	
30 g	Parmesan cheese, finely grated	**1 oz**
15 g	fresh wholemeal breadcrumbs	**½ oz**
1 tbsp	finely chopped parsley	**1 tbsp**

Preheat the oven to 220°C (425°F or Mark 7).

Plunge the spinach into a saucepan of boiling water for 30 seconds. Drain and refresh under cold running water. Squeeze the spinach dry, then chop it finely.

Heat the butter in a frying pan then add the spring onions and cook them gently until they are softened—2 to 3 minutes. Stir in the spinach and cook for 3 to 4 minutes. Season with black pepper.

Mix the topping ingredients together. Using a towel to protect your hands, carefully prise open the oysters using an oyster knife or other broad blade. Discard their flat half shells. With the oysters on their rounder half shells, divide the spinach mixture equally among them, spooning it neatly on top. Sprinkle the Parmesan topping evenly over the oysters.

Pour coarse salt into a large oven-proof dish to a depth of about 2.5 cm (1 inch). Place the oysters on the bed of salt and bake in the oven for 10 to 15 minutes, until they are golden-brown. Serve warm.

Seafood Sausages

Makes 30
sausages

Working
(and total)
time:
about 30
minutes

Per sausage:
Calories
25
Protein
2g
Cholesterol
10mg
Total fat
2g
Saturated fat
trace
Sodium
65mg

90 g	lemon sole fillet, skinned	**3 oz**
175 g	monkfish fillet	**6 oz**
125 g	salmon tailpiece fillet	**4 oz**
1	egg white	**1**
1 tsp	green peppercorns, coarsely crushed	**1 tsp**
$\frac{1}{4}$ tsp	grated lemon rind	**$\frac{1}{4}$ tsp**
1 tsp	salt	**1 tsp**
2 tbsp	virgin olive oil	**2 tbsp**
	lemon slices or wedges, for garnish	

Roughly chop the lemon sole, monkfish and half of the salmon. In a food processor, process the chopped fish for a few seconds, then add the egg white and process until the mixture becomes just paste-like. Chop the remaining salmon finely and mix it into the fish paste along with the peppercorns, lemon rind and salt.

Divide the fish paste into 30 walnut-sized portions and roll each piece into a sausage shape. Heat the oil in a heavy frying pan over medium heat until it is hot, but not smoking. Fry the sausages, turning all the time, until well browned—1$\frac{1}{2}$ to 2 minutes. Serve garnished with slices or wedges of lemon.

Ginger-Spiced Prawns

Makes 12 prawns
Working time: about 30 minutes
Total time: about 2 hours and 30 minutes (includes marinating)

Per prawn:
Calories 30
Protein 3g
Cholesterol 20mg
Total fat 2g
Saturated fat trace
Sodium 30mg

12	raw Mediterranean prawns (about 500 g/1 lb), gutted and butterflied	**12**	**2.5 cm**	piece fresh ginger root, peeled and finely chopped, or the juice extracted with a garlic press	**1 inch**
4 tbsp	low-sodium soy sauce or shoyu	**4 tbsp**	**½ tsp**	Chinese five-spice powder	**½ tsp**
2 tsp	fresh lemon or lime juice	**2 tsp**	**1 tbsp**	light sesame oil	**1 tsp**
2 tsp	honey	**2 tsp**		lettuce leaves, shredded	
1	garlic clove, finely chopped	**1**		lemon wedges, (optional)	

Combine the soy sauce, lemon or lime juice, honey, ginger, garlic and five-spice powder in a wide, shallow non-reactive dish. Place the butterflied prawns in this mixture, flesh side down, and leave to marinate in a cool place for 2 hours.

Preheat the grill to high, and brush a wide, fireproof pan with 1 teaspoon of the oil. Reserving the marinade, place the prawns, flesh side down, in the pan. Brush the shells of the prawns with the remaining oil and grill for 3 to 5 minutes, turning once, until the shells turn pink and the flesh is no longer translucent.

Meanwhile, reduce the reserved marinade in a small saucepan over high heat until only 1 tablespoon remains. Brush this glaze over both sides of the prawns. Serve immediately on a bed of the shredded lettuce, accompanied, if you like, with lemon wedges.

Mixed Seafood Pâté

Serves 20

Working time:
about 45
minutes

Total time:
about 3 hours
(Includes
marinating)

Calories
45

Protein
7g

Cholesterol
70mg

Total fat
1g

Saturated fat
1g

Sodium
200mg

250 g	smoked cod or haddock	8oz
½	lime, juice squeezed, rind grated	½
30 cl	unsalted fish stock, or water with two bay leaves, six peppercorns and 2 tbsp white wine vinegar added	½ pint
250 g	cod or haddock, skinned and boned	8 oz
125 g	soft herring roe	4 oz
½ tsp	light sesame oil	½ tsp
30 g	smoked cod's roe, skinned	1 oz

1 tbsp	chopped fresh dill	1 tsp
2 tbsp	anise-flavoured spirit	2 tbsp
2 tbsp	fromage frais or thick Greek yogurt	2 tbsp
2 tbsp	crème fraîche or soured cream	2 tbsp
¼ tsp	cayenne pepper	¼ tsp
	paprika	
	white pepper	
1 tsp	green peppercorns, crushed (optional)	1 tsp
2	lime slices, for garnish	2

Skin and roughly chop the smoked fish into 5 cm (2 inch) pieces. Marinate in the lime juice for 2 hours.

Meanwhile, bring the stock or flavoured water to the boil, then simmer the fresh fish gently until it flakes easily—3 to 5 minutes. Remove the fish from the pan and cool.

Wipe the soft roe with paper towels, discarding any dark veining or blood. Fry it gently in the sesame oil for 3 to 5 minutes, breaking it up gently as it cooks. Set aside to cool.

Drain and discard the marinade and flake the smoked fish. Reserve about one quarter of the fish, and place the rest in a blender. Flake the poached fish, reserve one quarter and place the rest in the blender or food processor. Add the soft and smoked roes, and process briefly. Blend in the remaining ingredients until smooth and then stir in the reserved flaked fish.

Spoon the seafood pâté into a serving dish. Garnish the top with a sprinkling of paprika, the lime slices and the dill sprig.

Smooth Potted Beef

Serves 12 as
a first course

Working time:
about 40
minutes

Total time:
about 8 hours
(includes
chilling)

Calories
160
Protein
30g
Cholesterol
60mg
Total fat
4g
Saturated fat
2g
Sodium
115mg

1.5 kg	topside of beef	3 lb
½ tsp	salt	¼ tsp
½ tsp	grated nutmeg	½ tsp
1½ tsp	ground allspice	1½ tsp
30 cl	unsalted veal stock	½ pint
1 tsp	powdered gelatine	1 tsp
	fresh thyme or parsley sprigs,	
	for garnish	

Preheat the oven to 200°C (400°F or Mark 6). Put the beef into a roasting pan and sprinkle it evenly with ¼ teaspoon of the salt. Roast the beef for 15 minutes, then reduce the oven temperature to 180°C (350°F or Mark 4) and continue roasting the meat for about 1¾ hours, basting it frequently, until it is well done. Transfer the beef to a plate, cover it loosely with foil and allow it to cool. Pour the pan juices into a bowl, allow them to cool for 30 minutes, then put them into the refrigerator until the fat rises to the surface and solidifies —about 2 hours. Remove the juices from the refrigerator and discard the layer of fat.

Cut away all fat from the roast beef, then cut the meat into small chunks. Put the chunks into a food processor and process them until the meat is finely minced. Add the nutmeg and allspice, the remaining salt, the roasting juices and 17.5 cl (6 fl oz) of the veal stock. Process the mixture to a smooth paste.

Spoon the beef paste into a serving dish. Press the paste down firmly, levelling and smoothing the top. Refrigerate the potted beef for 1 hour.

Meanwhile, dissolve the gelatine in 2 tablespoons of water. Quickly stir the dissolved gelatine into the remaining veal stock. Chill the stock until it begins to thicken, but is not yet set—about 30 minutes.

Pour the thickened stock evenly over the potted beef, then garnish it with the thyme or parsley sprigs. Refrigerate the potted beef for a further 2 to 3 hours, until it is well chilled.

Pink and Green Fish Terrine

Serves 16 as
a first course

Working time:
about 45
minutes

Total time:
about 4 hours
(includes
chilling)

Calories
50

Protein
7g

Cholesterol
30mg

Total fat
2g

Saturated fat
1g

Sodium
85mg

500 g	pink trout fillets, skinned	**1 lb**	
½ tsp	chopped wild fennel	**½ tsp**	
1½ tsp	chopped fresh dill	**1½ tsp**	
4	egg whites	**4**	
½ tsp	salt	**½ tsp**	
	white pepper		
15 g	unsalted butter	**½ oz**	
90 g	parsley, stalks removed	**3 oz**	
500 g	whiting or haddock fillets, skinned	**1 lb**	
1 tbsp	chopped fresh tarragon, or	**1 tbsp**	
	1 tsp dried tarragon		
1 tbsp	dry sherry or vermouth	**1 tbsp**	

Line a 20 by 6 by 7.5 cm (8 by 2½ by 3 inch) terrine or loaf tin with non-stick parchment paper.

Roughly chop the trout fillets, then purée them in a food processor. Add the fennel, dill, two of the egg whites, ¼ teaspoon of the salt and some white pepper, and blend again to form a smooth paste. Transfer the pink paste to the prepared terrine, smoothing it down with the back of a spoon, then make a groove lengthwise down the centre. Chill the paste while you prepare the green layer.

Preheat the oven to 190°C (375°F or Mark 5). Melt the butter in a small saucepan, add the parsley and gently cook until it is soft—about 10 minutes. Allow the parsley to cool, then place it in the food processor. Roughly chop the white fish and add it to the parsley. Process until they are well blended. Add the tarragon, the remaining egg whites, the sherry, the remaining salt and some white pepper. Process the mixture to a smooth purée. Transfer the purée to the terrine and smooth it into an even layer.

Cover the terrine loosely with non-stick parchment paper and stand it in a large roasting pan or dish. Pour boiling water into the roasting pan to come two thirds of the way up the side of the terrine. Bake the terrine until the mixture is set and firm to the touch—about 35 minutes. Leave to cool, then chill it for at least 2 hours. Turn out the terrine on to a platter, and serve it cut into slices.

Spinach and Crab Terrine

Serves 8 as a
first course

Working time:
about 40
minutes

Total time:
about 3 hours
(includes
chilling)

Calories
150
Protein
16g
Cholesterol
50mg
Total fat
7g
Saturated fat
1g
Sodium
300mg

250 g	spinach, washed and stemmed	**8 oz**
30 g	polyunsaturated margarine	**1 oz**
30 g	plain flour	**1 oz**
1	large crab, dressed, brown and white meat kept separate (about 500 g/1 lb crab meat)	**1**
	white pepper	
2 tbsp	fresh lemon juice	**2 tbsp**
30 cl	semi-skimmed milk	**½ tsp**
¼ tsp	salt	**¼ tsp**
3 tsp	powdered gelatine	**3 tsp**
	lemon wedges, for garnish	
	cucumber slices, for garnish	
	lettuce leaves for garnish	

Blanch the spinach in a large pan of boiling water for 1 minute. Drain and refresh it under cold running water. Gently press to remove all moisture. Chop the spinach in a blender.

Melt the margarine in a saucepan. Add the flour and cook it gently for 1 minute, stirring continuously. Gradually pour in the milk, still stirring, and cook over medium heat until the sauce boils. Reduce heat and simmer for 2 minutes. Stir in the salt and some pepper, then divide the sauce equally between two bowls. Add the white crab meat, the spinach and 1 tablespoon of the lemon juice to one bowl of sauce, and mix thoroughly. Add the brown crab meat and the remaining lemon juice to the second bowl, and mix well.

Dissolve the gelatine in 4 tablespoons of water. Divide this between the white and brown crab mixtures, and mix thoroughly.

Spoon half the white crab meat and spinach mixture into a greased 18 by 7.5 by 6 cm (7 by 3 by 2½inch) loaf tin and level it. Chill the tin in the refrigerator until the mixture is just setting—about 15 minutes. Spoon the brown crab meat mixture into the tin and level, then gently spoon the remaining white crab meat and spinach mixture over the brown crab meat. Chill the until firm—about 2 hours.

To unmould the terrine, dip the base in hot water for 5 seconds, then invert it on to a flat serving plate. Serve garnished with the lemon wedges, cucumber slices and lettuce leaves.

Quenelles with Rosé Wine Sauce

Serves 6

Working time:
about 45
minutes

Total time:
about 2 hours
and 30 minutes
(includes
chilling)

Calories
155
Protein
4g
Cholesterol
70mg
Total fat
8g
Saturated fat
3g
Sodium
95mg

350 g	skinless, boneless whiting fillet well chilled	12 oz
2	egg whites	2
$\frac{1}{8}$ tsp	grated nutmeg	$\frac{1}{8}$ tsp
$\frac{1}{8}$ tsp	cayenne pepper	$\frac{1}{8}$ tsp
$\frac{1}{4}$ tsp	salt	$\frac{1}{4}$ tsp
	white pepper	
125 g	crème fraîche	4 oz
175 g	fromage frais	6 oz

	Rosé wine sauce	
1 tbsp	safflower oil	1 tbsp
1	shallot, finely chopped	1
175 g	tomatoes, skinned, seeded and chopped	6 oz
30 cl	rosé wine	$\frac{1}{2}$ pint
2 tbsp	fromage frais	2 tbsp
$\frac{1}{4}$ tsp	salt	$\frac{1}{4}$ tsp
	freshly ground black pepper	

Put the fish, egg whites, nutmeg, cayenne pepper, salt and some white pepper in a food processor and blend to a smooth paste. Blend in the *crème fraîche* and the *fromage frais*, a little at a time. Turn into a bowl, cover, and refrigerate for about 2 hours.

Heat the oil in a small saucepan and cook the shallot gently for 30 seconds. Stir in the tomatoes and wine, boil and cook, stirring occasionally, until the liquid is reduced to about 35 cl (12 fl oz)—about 8 minutes. Set the sauce aside.

Shape 12 quenelles from the fish mixture using two large spoons. Place them, not touching, in a wide pan. Pour boiling water down the side of the pan, until the quenelles are just covered, and simmer gently until just firm—about 10 minutes.

Meanwhile, reheat the sauce over low heat. Stir in half of the *fromage frais* and season. Mix 1 tablespoon of the wine sauce with the remaining *fromage frais*. Distribute the rest of the sauce among six heated serving plates.

Create a marbled effect with the two sauces on six plates. Lift the quenelles from the pan with a slotted spoon. Serve two on each plate.

Baby Beetroot and Blackcurrant Moulds

Serves 6

Working time: about 55 minutes

Total time: about 1 hour and 45 minutes (includes setting and chilling)

Calories 65
Protein 4g
Cholesterol 5mg
Total fat 2g
Saturated fat 1g
Sodium 35mg

10	baby beetroots, washed but not peeled, tops trimmed off (about 500 g/1 lb)	10
60 cl	blackcurrant juice	1 pint
	gelatine	

Lime-yogurt sauce

250 g	thick Greek yogurt	8 oz
2	limes, juice and finely grated rind	2
	freshly ground black pepper	

In a saucepan, cook the beetroots in enough boiling water to cover them until they are tender—about 25 minutes. Drain and leave until they are cool enough to handle, then peel them while they are still warm. Reserve five of the beetroots, and use a sharp knife to slice the remainder thinly. Divide the slices between six 12.5 cl (4 fl oz) jelly moulds.

In a non-reactive saucepan, bring the blackcurrant juice to the boil. Remove it from the heat and sprinkle the powdered gelatine over the hot liquid. When the gelatine has dissolved completely, pour the blackcurrant mixture into the moulds. Refrigerate the beetroot until the jelly has set—about 1 hour.

Meanwhile, prepare the lime-yogurt sauce.

Place the Greek yogurt in a bowl. Add the lime rind and juice, and beat them into the yogurt with a small whisk. Chill the sauce in the refrigerator.

To unmould the jellies, dip the base of each mould into a pan of boiling water for a couple of seconds and then turn it out on to a serving plate. Slice the reserved beetroots, arrange them round each mould, and serve immediately, accompanied by the lime-yogurt sauce.

Editor's Note: The blackcurrant juice renders the jelly fairly tart. For a less tart jelly, apple juice can be substituted for half of the blackcurrant juice.

Carrot and Herb Ramekins

Serves 4 as a
first course

Working time:
about 30
minutes

Total time:
about 1 hour

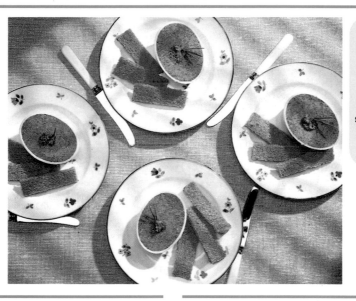

Calories
120

Protein
2g

Cholesterol
0mg

Total fat
9g

Saturated fat
2g

Sodium
410mg

30 g	parsley	**1 oz**
30 g	chives	**1 oz**
45 g	polyunsaturated margarine	**1½ oz**
500 g	carrots, thinly sliced	**1 lb**
	garlic clove, finely chopped	
2 tsp	balsamic or sherry vinegar	**2 tsp**

½ tsp	grated lemon rind	**½ tsp**
1 tbsp	fresh lemon juice	**1 tbsp**
½ tsp	ground cumin	**½ tsp**
½ tsp	salt	**½ tsp**
	freshly ground black pepper	

Set aside four small parsley sprigs and a few chives for garnish. Chop the remainder.

Melt the margarine in a heavy-bottomed saucepan over medium heat. Add the carrots and cook them, covered, until they soften—about 10 minutes—stirring them occasionally to prevent them from burning When they are almost cooked, add the garlic, vinegar, lemon rind and juice, and the cumin. Stir the contents of the pan well and continue cooking for a further 2 minutes. Add the

chopped parsley and chives to the pan, stirring them in thoroughly.

Transfer the mixture to a food processor or blender and add the salt and some freshly ground black pepper. Process the ingredients to a purée. Spoon the purée into four individual ramekins and chill them in the refrigerator until the pâté has set—at least 30 minutes. Decorate the pâté with the reserved parsley sprigs and chives before serving.

Anchovy and Lentil Dip

Serves 6 as a
first course

Working
time: about
15 minutes

Total time
about 1 hour

Calories
180
Protein
13g
Cholesterol
10mg
Total fat
2g
Saturated fat
trace
Sodium
450mg

250 g	red lentils, picked over and rinsed	**8 oz**
1 or 2	garlic cloves, finely chopped	**1 or 2**
1	large onion, chopped	**1**
60 g	anchovy fillets, soaked in a little milk for 15 minutes to reduce their saltiness	**2 oz**

60 cl	unsalted vegetable stock	**1 pint**
2 tbsp	fresh lemon juice	**2 tbsp**
30 g	dry breadcrumbs	**1 oz**
	chives, for garnish	
	lemon slices, cut into pieces, for garnish	

Place the lentils, chopped garlic and onion, and the vegetable stock in a heavy-bottomed saucepan. Bring the stock to the boil and skim off any scum that rises to the surface. Reduce the heat, cover and cook the lentils until they are soft and have absorbed all the stock—about 30 minutes. If any of the stock remains at the end of this time, cook the lentils uncovered over medium heat, stirring constantly, until the moisture has evaporated.

Pat the anchovies dry on paper towels and place them in a food processor or blender with the cooked lentils, the lemon juice and the breadcrumbs. Process the ingredients until they are smooth. Divide the mixture among six individual ramekins and leave to cool. Just before serving, garnish each portion with a few chives and pieces of lemon.

Gemelli with Tomatoes, Rosemary and Thyme

Serves 8 as
an appetizer

Working time:
about 25
minutes

Total time:
about 30
minutes

Calories
175
Protein
5g
Cholesterol
5mg
Total fat
6g
Saturated fat
1g
Sodium
250mg

250 g	gemelli (or short tubular pasta)	8 oz	2 tbsp	virgin olive oil	2 tbsp
60 g	sun-dried tomatoes packed in oil, drained and thinly sliced	2 oz	½ tsp	salt	½ tsp
				freshly ground black pepper	
4	small leeks, trimmed, cleaned and cut into 2 cm (¾ inch) slices	4	1 tsp	fresh thyme, or ¼ tsp dried thyme	1 tsp
2	shallots, finely chopped	2	4 tbsp	dry white wine	4 tbsp
1 tsp	fresh rosemary, or ¼ tsp dried rosemary	1 tsp	4 tbsp	freshly grated Parmesan cheese	4 tbsp
1½ tbsp	fresh lemon juice	1½ tbsp			

Precook the gemelli in 3 litres (5 pints) of unsalted boiling water for 2 minutes—the pasta will be underdone. Drain it and put it in a large fireproof casserole. Stir in the tomatoes, ¼ litre (8 fl oz) of water, 45g (1¼oz) of the white part of the leeks, the shallots, rosemany, lemon juice, 1 tablespoon of the oil, ¼ teaspoon salt and some pepper. Cover the casserole and cook the mixture over low heat, stirring occasionally, until all the liquid has been absorbed—about 8 minutes.

Meanwhile, in a large frying pan, gently heat the remaining tablespoon of oil. Add the remaining leek slices, the remaining salt,

some pepper and the thyme. Cook the mixture for 3 minutes, stirring from time to time. Raise the heat and cook for 1 minute more, then pour in the wine. Cook until the liquid has evaporated—about 4 minutes.

Add the leek mixture to the casserole, then stir in the cheese. To infuse the pasta with the flavours of the herbs and sun-dried tomatoes, cover the casserole and let it stand for 5 minutes before serving.

Editor's Note: Two tablespoons of the oil from the sun-dried tomatoes may be substituted for the olive oil called for here.

Green-Jacket Dublin Bay Prawns

<table>
<tr><td>Makes 12
prawns

Working
(and total)
time: about
40 minutes</td><td></td><td>Per prawn
Calories
30
Protein
4g
Cholesterol
25mg
Total fat
0g
Saturated fat
0g
Sodium
200mg</td></tr>
</table>

12	fresh or frozen Dublin Bay prawns (about 750g/1 lb)	12
12	large spinach leaves	12
3 tbsp	low-sodium soy sauce or shoyu	3 tbsp
3 tbsp	mirin	3 tbsp
	Poaching liquid	
15 cl	dry white wine	¼ pint
1	onion or shallot, sliced	1

1	carrot, diced	1
2	sticks celery, diced	2
1	bay leaf fresh or dry	1
5	parsley sprigs	5
2	fresh thyme, dill or wild fennel sprigs	2
1 tsp	salt	1 tsp
5	black peppercorns	5

For the poaching liquid pour 1.5 to 2 litres (2½ to 3½ pints) of water into a large fireproof casserole and add the wine, onion, carrot, celery, bay leaf, herbs, salt and peppercorns. Bring the liquid to the boil, and simmer for 10 minutes. Rinse the prawns, then put them in the liquid; cover the casserole and simmer for 5 to 8 minutes.

While the prawns are cooking, prepare the spinach leaves. Wash the leaves thoroughly, blanch them for 30 seconds in boiling water, then refresh them under cold running water and drain. Remove the central rib from each leaf and fold lengthwise to form a ribbon about half as wide as the length of a prawn.

When cooked, rinse and twist off the heads, legs and front claws, and discard. Using a sharp pair of scissors, slit the underside of the shell along the belly up to the tail fins. Using a sharp knife, remove the dark vein. Remove most of the shell leaving only the tail fins intact.

Combine the soy sauce and mirin in a small bowl, and dip each prawn in the mixture. Wrap the end opposite the tail in a spinach leaf ribbon, leaving the tail fins and a little of the body exposed. (The spinach will adhere to itself.)

Arrange the prawns on a serving dish. Serve the remaining soy sauce and mirin mixture as a dip.

Beef and Tofu Satay

Serves 12

Working time:
about 45
minutes

Total time:
about 5 hours
(includes
marinating)

Calories
145
Protein
7g
Cholesterol
10mg
Total fat
8g
Saturated fat
2g
Sodium
20mg

3 tbsp	low-sodium soy sauce	**3 tbsp**
3 tbsp	fresh lemon juice	**3 tbsp**
1	garlic clove, finely chopped	**1**
1cm	fresh ginger root, chopped	**½ inch**
½ tsp	light brown sugar	**½ tsp**
¼ tsp	hot red pepper flakes	**¼ tsp**
250 g	beef fillet, cubed	**8 oz**
250 g	firm tofu, well drained, cubed	**8 oz**
	fresh coriander leaves, for garnish	

Peanut sauce

60 g	shelled peanuts	**2 oz**
2 tbsp	ground nut oil	**2 tbsp**
1	onion, very finely chopped	**1**
1	garlic clove, crushed	**1**
¾ tsp	chili powder	**¾ tsp**
¾ tsp	ground coriander	**¾ tsp**
1 tsp	light brown sugar	**1 tsp**
2 tsp	fresh lemon juice	**2 tsp**
2 tsp	low-sodium soy sauce or shoyu	**2 tsp**
1 tsp	cornflour	**1 tsp**

Mix the soy sauce, lemon juice, garlic, ginger, sugar and red pepper flakes. Marinate the beef and tofu in this mixture for 4 to 6 hours.

Preheat the oven to 180°C (350°F or Mark 4). Spread the peanuts on a baking sheet and toast in the oven for 10 minutes. Rub them in a tea towel to remove their skins. Grind them in a food processor.

Fry the onion, garlic, ground peanuts, chili powder and coriander, in the oil for 2 minutes, stirring. Add the brown sugar, lemon juice, soy sauce and ¼ litre (8 fl oz) of water,

and boil, stirring. Simmer to a creamy consistency—about 10 minutes. Place the cornflour in a bowl, add 1 tablespoon of water and stir to a paste. When the sauce is ready, stir in the cornflour paste. Cool in a serving dish.

Soak 12 bamboo skewers in cold water for 30 minutes and then dry them.

Thread the beef and the tofu cubes alternately on to the skewers and grill them 8 to 10 cm below the heat source, turning occasionally—5 to 7 minutes. Serve the satay hot, accompanied by the peanut sauce.

Fresh and Smoked Mackerel Pâté

Serves 10
as a first
course

Total 1 hour
and 30
minutes
(includes
chilling)

Calories
145
Protein
14g
Cholesterol
40mg
Total fat
10g
Saturated fat
3g
Sodium
265mg

350 g	fresh mackerel, filleted and skinned	12 oz		juice of half, the other half cut into wedges chopped	
250 g	smoked mackerel fillets, skin and any bones removed	8 oz	1 tbsp	chopped fresh dill or fennel tops, plus whole sprigs for garnish	1 tbsp
250 g	low-fat fromage frais	8 oz		freshly ground black pepper	
1	lemon, grated rind and	1			

Pour water into a saucepan to fill it to a depth of 2.5 cm (1 inch) Set a vegetable steamer in the pan and bring the water to the boil. Put the fresh mackerel in the steamer, cover the pan tightly and steam the fish until it is cooked—about 10 minutes.

Place the cooked fresh mackerel and the smoked mackerel in a food processor or blender, together with all but 1½ tablespoons of the *fromage frais*, the lemon rind and juice,

and the chopped dill or fennel, and process the ingredients to a smooth paste. Season the pate with some pepper. Transfer the pâté to a bowl, cover it and chill it for at least 1 hour

Remove the pâté from the refrigerator just before serving, stir it and divide it among 10 individual ramekins. Garnish each portion witn a little of the reserved *fromage frais* and the dill or fennel sprigs, and serve immediately with the wedges of lemon.

Parcels of Spring Vegetables with Lemon Butter

Serves 4

Working time:
about 40
minutes

Total time:
about 1 hour

Calories
70
Protein
3g
Cholesterol
20mg
Total fat
6g
Saturated fat
4g
Sodium
70mg

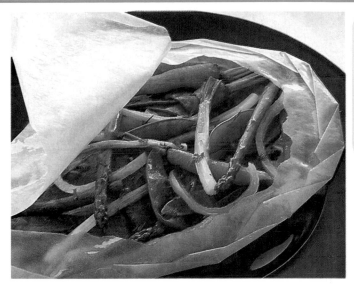

16	small young carrots, scraped with green tops partly retained	16	4 tsp	thinly cut chives	4 tsp
			4 tsp	chopped fresh chervil	4 tsp
150 g	mange-tout topped and tailed, strings removed	5 oz	4 tsp	chopped fresh tarragon	4 tsp
				Lemon butter	
20	thin asparagus spears, trimmed	20	30 g	unsalted butter, softened	1 oz
12	spring onions, trimmed and cut into lengths	12	1 tsp	grated lemon rind	1 tsp
			1 tsp	fresh lemon juice	1 tsp
1	sweet yellow pepper, seeded, deribbed, cut into strips	1	$\frac{1}{8}$ tsp	salt	$\frac{1}{8}$ tsp
				freshly ground black pepper	

In a small bowl, mix together all the ingredients for the lemon butter, cover with plastic film and put in the refrigerator to chill. Preheat the oven to 220°C (425°F or Mark 7).

Fill a saucepan with about 2.5 cm (1 inch) of water. Put a steamer in the pan and bring the water to the boil. Add the carrots, cover them tightly and steam them until they are partially cooked, but still firm—about 8 minutes. Drain and transfer them to a large bowl. Toss in the mange-tout, asparagus, spring onions and pepper.

Cut out four circles about 25 cm (10 inches) in diameter from parchment paper Fold each in half, crease, then open out. Brush each circle lightly with oil. Spoon a quarter of the vegetables on to a circle, keeping the filling to one side of the crease and forming a neat rectangle lying parallel to the fold. Dot the vegetables with a little lemon butter, sprinkle them with 1 teaspoon of each of the herbs and fold over to enclose the filling. Crimp the edges of the paper, in overlapping double folds, to seal. Repeat for the other three.

Brush the packages with a little oil to prevent them from becoming soggy in the oven. Place the parcels on a baking sheet and bake them for 12 minutes before serving.

Smoked Salmon Parcels with a Pink Trout Filling

Serves 8 as a first course

Working time about 45 minutes

Total time: about 4 hours (includes chilling)

Calories 120
Protein 19g
Cholesterol 40mg
Total fat 5g
Saturated fat 1g
Sodium 370mg

400 g	pink trout fillets	**14 oz**
¼	onion, chopped	**¼**
2	lemon slices	**2**
1	bay leaf	**1**
6	black peppercorns	**6**
175 g	low-fat fromage frais	**6 oz**
⅛ tsp	salt	**⅛ tsp**
	freshly ground black pepper	
⅛ tsp	ground coriander	**⅛ tsp**
2 tsp	powdered gelatine	**2 tsp**
1 tbsp	fresh lemon juice	**1 tbsp**
1 tbsp	cut chives, plus 16 long chives	**1 tbsp**
1	egg white	**1**
125 g	smoked salmon, cut into eight	**4 oz**
	16 by 5 cm (6 ½ by 2 inch) rectangles	
	curly endive, for garnish (optional)	

Lay the trout fillets in a frying pan. Add the onion, lemon slices, bay leaf and peppercorns, then pour in enough water to barely cover the fish. Bring to the boil, reduce the heat and cover. Simmer gently until cooked—7 to 10 minutes. Leave fish to cool in the liquid. Meanwhile, line a 20 by 10 by 5 cm (8 by 4 by 2 inch) loaf tin with parchment paper.

Lift the cooled trout fillets from the pan and discard the liquid. Flake the fish finely, discarding the skin and bones. Place the flaked trout in a bowl and beat in the *fromage frais*, the salt, a little pepper and the ground coriander. Dissolve the gelatine in the lemon juice and 2 tablespoons of water. Stir this into

the trout mixture and add the cut chives. Whisk the egg white until stiff and beat 2 tablespoons into the fish mixture, then fold in the remaining egg white, distributing it evenly. Turn the mousse into the prepared tin and chill it until firmly set—at least 3 hours.

Turn the mousse out of the tin and remove the paper. Cut it into eight even-sized blocks whose lengths are the width of the smoked salmon rectangles. Wrap each portion in a piece of salmon, leaving the ends of the mousse exposed. Pass two chives round the long and short dimensions of the parcel respectively, and lightly knot together. Serve, garnished with lemon slices and a curly endive.

Soused Trout with Apple

Serves 4

Working time:
about 45
minutes

Total time:
about 2 hours
and 30 minutes
(includes
chilling)

Calories
120
Protein
15g
Cholesterol
30mg
Total fat
3g
Saturated fat
1g
Sodium
100mg

2	trout, filleted	2
30 g	fresh wholemeal breadcrumbs	1 oz
$\frac{1}{2}$	lemon, grated rind and juice	$\frac{1}{2}$
2 tsp	chopped fresh dill	2 tsp
	freshly ground black pepper	
1	small onion, thinly sliced	1
1	bayleaf	1

3	cloves	3
1	small blade mace	1
4	black peppercorns	4
6 tbsp	cider vinegar	6 tbsp
1	red dessert apple	1
1	green dessert apple	1

Preheat the oven to 190°C (375°F or Mark 5).

In a small bowl, combine the fresh breadcrumbs, the grated lemon rind and all but 1 teaspoon of the juice, the chopped dill, and some black pepper. Lay the trout fillets flat on the work surface, skin side down. Spoon a little of the breadcrumb mixture on each of the trout pieces and roll up the fish, starting from the tail end, to enclose the bread filling. Secure the stuffed rolls with cocktail sticks.

Arrange the onion slices in the base of an ovenproof dish. Add the bay leaf, cloves, mace and peppercorns, and arrange the trout in one layer on top of the onions and spices.

Mix the cider vinegar with 6 tablespoons of water and pour this liquid over the fish. Cover the baking dish with foil and bake for 30 minutes. Remove the dish from the oven, let the fish rolls cool to room temperature, then refrigerate them in their cooking liquid for at least 1 hour before serving.

To serve the soused trout, remove the cocktail sticks and cut the fish rolls into 2.5 cm (1 inch) slices with a sharp knife. Core, halve and thinly slice the apples. Toss the slices in the remaining lemon juice to prevent discolouration. Serve the fish with the spiced onion from the baking dish and the apple slices.

Steamed Cucumber with Herb and Yogurt Sauce

Serves 4

Working (and total) time: about 20 minutes

Calories
50
Protein
3g
Cholesterol
0mg
Total fat
3g
Saturated fat
2g
Sodium
40mg

1	large cucumber	1	
	freshly ground black pepper		
250 g	thick Greek yogurt	8 oz	
1 tbsp	chopped fresh dill	1 tbsp	

1 tbsp	chopped parsley	1 tbsp	
½ tbsp	chopped fresh tarragon	½ tbsp	
4	fresh tarragon sprigs	4	

With a sharp knife, peel the cucumber and chop it into 2.5 cm (1 inch) pieces. Remove the seeds from the centre of each piece with an apple corer. Pour enough water into a saucepan to fill it about 2.5 cm (1 inch) deep. Set a vegetable steamer in the pan and bring the water to the boil. Place the cucumber pieces in the steamer, season with some black pepper, cover the saucepan and steam until the cucumber is just heated through—3 to 4 minutes.

While the cucumber is steaming, prepare the sauce by mixing together the Greek yogurt, dill, parsley and chopped tarragon in a small saucepan. Heat the mixture over very low heat until the yogurt is warm, but not hot—about 1 minute.

Using a slotted spoon, transfer the cucumber pieces to warmed plates. Garnish the cucumber with the tarragon sprigs and serve with the warm yogurt sauce.

Lemon Sole Paupiettes with Ginger and Dill

Serves 4 as
a starter

Working
(and total)
time: about
45 minutes

Calories
230

Protein
32g

Cholesterol
95mg

Total fat
9g

Saturated fat
4g

Sodium
370mg

2	large lemon soles (about 500 to 750 g/1 to 1½ lb each)	2
30 g	unsalted butter, softened	1 oz
15 g	fresh ginger root, peeled and very finely chopped	½ oz
1½ tbsp	chopped fresh dill	1½ tbsp
¼ tsp	salt	¼ tsp
	freshly ground black pepper	
1 tsp	lemon juice	1 tsp
500 g	courgettes, cut into julienne strips	1 lb
1 tsp	cornflour	1 tsp
	lemon twists for garnish	

Skin and fillet the soles. Trim the 'frilly' edge from each fillet to neaten, then roughly chop the trimmings and set aside. Blend the butter with the chopped ginger, 1 tablespoon of the dill, the salt, pepper and lemon juice. Mix in the reserved sole trimmings.

Lay the sole fillets on the work surface skinned-side uppermost, then spread each one with ginger and dill butter. Roll up each fillet, from head to tail, to enclose the butter and form a neat paupiette. Place the paupiettes in a shallow dish. Loosely cover the dish with plastic film, and set aside.

Place the courgettes in another shallow dish, then season with salt and pepper. Cover the dish with plastic film, pulling back one corner to vent. Microwave the courgettes on high for 5 to 6 minutes, until they are barely cooked. Cover and keep warm while the sole is cooking.

With the microwave on high, cook the paupiettes for 4 to 5 minutes, turning them half way through cooking. Carefully arrange the paupiettes and courgettes on a hot serving dish. Cover and keep warm.

Blend the cornflour with a little cold water. Stir the cornflour into the fish juices, then microwave on high for 1½ minutes until the sauce thickens, whisking every 30 seconds. Glaze the paupiettes with the sauce, garnish with the remaining, and lemon twists. Serve immediately.

Roast Beef and Radicchio on Rye Bread

·Serves 4

Working
(and total)
time: about
25 minutes

Calories
195
Protein
13g
Cholesterol
40mg
Total fat
10g
Saturated fat
4g
Sodium
60mg

175 g	new potatoes	**6 oz**
15 g	unsalted butter, softened	**½ oz**
4	thin slices dark rye bread	**4**
12	radicchio leaves, washed and dried	**12**
175 g	rare roast beef, trimmed of fat and thinly sliced	**6 oz**

	Mustard dressing	
2 tsp	walnut oil	**2 tsp**
1 tsp	red wine vinegar	**1 tsp**
⅛ tsp	sugar	**⅛ tsp**
1 tsp	grainy mustard	**1 tsp**
	freshly ground black pepper	

Scrub the potatoes and cook them in boiling water until they are cooked but still show resistance when pierced with the tip of a knife—about 10 minutes. Drain them well and leave to cool.

While the potatoes are cooking, mix all the dressing ingredients together in a small bowl and set aside. Spread the butter thinly on the bread and arrange three radicchio leaves on each slice.

Slice the potatoes and divide them among the open sandwiches. Fold the slices of beef and arrange them on top of the potatoes. Spoon a little dressing over each open sandwich and serve.

Aubergine Pâté

Serves 6 as a first course

Working time: about 8 minutes

Total time: about 50 minutes

Calories 60
Protein 2g
Cholesterol trace
Total fat 4g
Saturated fat 1g
Sodium 75mg

3	large aubergines (about 1.5 kg/3 lb)	3
4 tbsp	fresh lemon juice	4 tbsp
6 tbsp	plain low-fat yogurt	6 tbsp
3 tbsp	tahini	3 tbsp
$\frac{1}{8}$ tsp	salt	$\frac{1}{8}$ tsp
2	garlic cloves, finely chopped	2

Prick the aubergines in several places with a skewer or the tip of a sharp knife. and place them in the microwave oven on a double thickness of paper towels. Microwave the aubergines on high for about 9 minutes, turning them over half way through the cooking time. When cooked, the aubergines should be soft right through. Set them aside until they have cooled enough to handle. Cut each aubergine in half and scoop out the soft flesh, then set the flesh aside in a bowl to cool completely—about 30 minutes.

Purée the aubergine flesh in a food processor or blender, together with the lemon juice, yogurt, tahini, salt and garlic. Transfer the purée to a bowl and sprinkle it with paprika before serving.

Oriental Fish Parcels

Serves 4

Working
(and total)
time: about
20 minutes

Calories
80
Protein
11g
Cholesterol
35mg
Total fat
3g
Saturated fat
1g
Sodium
85mg

150 g	carrots, cut into fine julienne	5 oz		300 g	white fish fillet (such as cod,	10 oz
3	spring onions, cut	3			or haddock), skinned	
	into fine julienne				freshly ground black pepper	
2 tsp	chopped fresh coriander	2 tsp		1	lime, cut into thin wedges,	1
2 tsp	sesame oil	2 tsp			for garnish	

Cut out four 25 cm (10 inch) squares of greaseproof paper. In a small bowl, mix together the carrot and spring onion strips and the chopped coriander. Divide the mixture of vegetables and herbs equally among the paper squares.

With a sharp knife, slice the fish thinly into strips and divide the strips evenly among the squares. Sprinkle each portion with the sesame oil and some freshly ground black pepper.

Fold a paper square to enclose the fish and vegetables. Bring two sides of the square up over the filling, allowing one side to overlap the other. Fold over a margin of about 1 cm (½ inch) on both remaining sides. Fold each of the margins over once again to enclose the packet completely, pressing down on the creases to seal them. Repeat the process to wrap the remaining three parcels. Arrange the fish parcels in a single layer on a steamer rack.

Place the rack over boiling water, cover the pan and steam the fish parcels for 5 minutes Place each parcel, still wrapped, on a serving dish, and garnish with wedges of lime.

Roulade of Salmon and Sole Filled with Spinach

Makes about
35 slices

Working time:
about 45
minutes

Total time:
about 4 hours
(includes
chilling)

Per slice
Calories
30
Protein
4g
Cholesterol
15mg
Total fat
2g
Saturated fat
trace
Sodium
70mg

350 g	middle cut salmon	12 oz
300 g	Doversole or plaice fillets	10 oz
350 g	spinach washed and stemmed	12 oz
1	lemon, roughly sliced	1
1	onion, roughly chopped	1
2	carrots, roughly sliced	2

2 tsp	black peppercorns	2 tsp
30 g	parsley sprigs	1 oz
45 cl	white wine vinegar	¾ pint
1 tsp	chopped fresh dill	1 tsp
1 tsp	salt	1 tsp
2.5 litres	unsalted fish stock or water	4 pints

Cut the salmon in half lengthwise and remove all the bones; trim any membrane. Cut thin horizontal slices from each half, working towards the skin. In the centre of a large piece of wet muslin, lay the slices of salmon to form a rectangle measuring 35 by 20 cm (14 by 8 inches). Slice the sole in the same way and lay on top of the salmon.

Cook the spinach for 1 minute in boiling water, drain, squeeze dry and chop it. Arrange the spinach along one long edge of the fish rectangle in a cylinder about 2 cm (¾ inch) in diameter.

Grip the edge of the muslin nearest the spinach. Pull the muslin towards you and gently lift it, gradually rolling the fish round

the spinach until the roll is complete. Wrap the muslin round the roll and secure it at each end with string. Tie 2.5 cm (1 inch) wide strips of muslin round the roll at intervals of about 5 cm (2 inches).

To prepare a court-bouillon, place the lemon, onion, carrots, peppercorns, parsley, vinegar, dill and salt in a fish kettle. Add enough fish stock to cover the roll when it is put in the pan. Bring to the boil, then reduce the heat until it is just simmering. Carefully place the roll in the court-bouillon and poach for 3 to 4 minutes. Take the fish kettle off the heat and cool. Then place in the refrigerator to chill thoroughly—at least 3 hours, before unwrapping and serving.

Jellied Lemon Chicken

Serves 12 as a main course

Working time: about 45 minutes

Total time: about 15 hours (includes chilling)

Calories 140
Protein 26g
Cholesterol 70mg
Total fat 4g
Saturated fat 2g
Sodium 170mg

3 kg	chicken, giblets reserved except for the liver	**6½ lb**
3	lemons, one quartered, the grated rind only of two	**3**
1	onion, roughly chopped	**1**
2	carrots, roughly chopped	**2**
2	sticks celery, roughly chopped	**2**
60 g	parsley, finely chopped, plus one parsley sprig	**2 oz**
1 tsp	salt	**1 tsp**
8	black peppercorns freshly ground black pepper	**8**
4 tsp	capers	**4 tsp**

Rinse the chicken and giblets well under cold running water and pat them dry. Put the lemon quarters inside the chicken. Place the chicken and giblets in a large pan and pour in 60 cl (1 pint) of cold water. Add the onion, carrots, celery, parsley sprig, ½ teaspoon salt and the peppercorns. Bring the liquid to the boil over medium heat, then let simmer, partially covered, until the chicken is cooked and the juices run clear when a thigh is pierced with a skewer—1½ to 2 hours. Remove the chicken from the pan, partially cover it with foil and set it aside.

Strain the stock with a muslin-lined sieve into a heatproof bowl; discard the solids. Let the stock cool for about 1 hour, then chill it for 3 to 4 hours, until the fat rises to the surface and solidifies and the stock becomes jellied. Discard the fat. Stand the bowl in hot water until the stock becomes liquid again.

Meanwhile, remove the flesh from the chicken, discarding the skin and bones, and cut it into 2.5 cm (1 inch) cubes. Place one third of the cubes in a large, round serving bowl and add a little of the remaining salt and some pepper. Sprinkle on one third each of the capers, chopped parsley and grated lemon rind. Repeat twice more, ending with a layer of capers, parsley and lemon rind. Carefully pour the stock into the bowl to cover the chicken completely. Cover the bowl and chill overnight before serving.

Wine-Glazed Red Mullet

Serves 4

Working (and total) time: about 45 minutes

Calories 140
Protein 13g
Cholesterol 25mg
Total fat 6g
Saturated fat 1g
Sodium 160mg

1	large red mullet (300 g/10 oz), cleaned and filleted but not skinned	1
¼ tsp	salt	¼ tsp
	freshly ground black pepper	
4 tbsp	red wine	4 tbsp
½	small red onion	½
6	pink or black peppercorns	6
2 tbsp	red wine vinegar	2 tbsp
2 tsp	light unrefined granulated sugar	2 tsp
125 g	red grapes, halved and seeded	4 oz
2	small hearts of radicchio, quartered	2
1 tbsp	grapeseed or safflower oil	1 tbsp

Remove the fine bones from the centre of the fish fillet with tweezers. Season the skin-free side of each mullet fillet lightly with salt and ground pepper, and set them aside

Boil then simmer the wine, onion and peppercorns until reduced to 2 tablespoons. Discard the onion and the peppercorns. Add the wine vinegar and sugar to the saucepan and cook rapidly until reduced to about 2 tablespoons of syrupy glaze. Preheat the grill.

Set aside 1 teaspoon of the glaze for salad dressing and coat the skin sides of the fillets with half of the glaze from the saucepan, keeping the remainder in the pan. Brush the grill pan and rack with a little oil and arrange

the fish on the rack, skin side facing upwards.

Whisk together the oil and the reserved teaspoon of glaze to form the salad dressing. Toss the grapes and radicchio quarters in this mixture and place them in a fireproof dish, ready to heat through under the grill.

Grill the red mullet, skin side upwards, close to the heat source—never allowing the skin to blister—for 3 to 5 minutes. After two minutes, brush with the remaining glaze.

Remove from the grill and set aside. Heat the salad for about 30 seconds under the grill.

Slice each fillet diagonally into three or four pieces. Arrange on individual plates with the warm salad, and serve immediately.

Water Chestnut Fritters

Serves 6 as
an appetizer

Working time:
about 30
minutes

Total time:
about 45
minutes

Calories
125
Protein
5g
Cholesterol
10mg
Total fat
6g
Saturated fat
1g
Sodium
128mg

500 g	fresh water chestnuts	1 lb
1 tsp	sugar, dissolved in 1 litre (1¾ pints) cold water	1 tsp
90 g	uncooked chicken breast meat, coarsely chopped	3 oz
125 g	mushrooms, stemmed	4 oz
1	spring onion, chopped	1
2 tbsp	finely chopped ginger root	2 tbsp
1	garlic clove, finely chopped	1

1 tbsp	low-sodium soy sauce, or naturally fermented shoyu	1 tbsp
2 tbsp	peanut oil	2 tbsp
	Ginger-garlic dip	
1 tbsp	finely chopped fresh ginger root	1 tbsp
1	garlic clove, finely chopped	1
12.5 cl	rice vinegar	4 floz
½ tsp	dark sesame oil	½ tsp
6	thin carrot rounds	6

Peel the water chestnuts with a small, sharp knife, and drop them into the sugared water as you work. (The sugar will help preserve the water chestnuts' natural sweetness.)

Preheat the oven to 180°C (350°F or Mark 4). Put the chicken, mushrooms, spring onion, ginger, garlic and soy sauce in a food processor or blender. Purée the mixture, stopping occasionally to scrape down the sides, until it is smooth—about 4 minutes. Transfer the purée to a mixing bowl. Chop the chestnuts coarsely and combine them with the purée. With your hands, mould the mixture into balls about 2.5 cm (1 inch) in

diameter (there will be 25 to 30 of these).

Heat the peanut oil in a large, shallow fireproof casserole over medium-high heat. Brown the fritters on one side for about 2 minutes. Turn them over and put the casserole in the oven. Bake the fritters until they are browned and cooked through—5 to 7 minutes.

Meanwhile, make the dipping sauce. Whisk together the ginger, garlic, vinegar and sesame oil in a small bowl. Float the carrot rounds on top.

Arrange the fritters on a platter and serve them with the ginger-garlic dip.

Oyster Mushroom Ramekins

Serves 4

Working time:
about 20
minutes

Total time:
about 35
minutes

Calories
45
Protein
3g
Cholesterol
55mg
Total fat
3g
Saturated fat
1g
Sodium
75mg

1 tsp	safflower oil	1 tsp
1	small onion, finely chopped	1
2 tsp	chopped fresh chervil	2 tsp
250 g	oyster mushrooms, finely chopped	8 oz

1	egg, separated, plus one egg white	1
1 tbsp	double cream	1 tbsp
⅛ tsp	salt	⅛ tsp
	freshly ground black pepper	
	fresh chervil sprigs, for garnish	

Preheat the oven to 180°C (350°F or Mark 4).

In a heavy-bottomed saucepan, heat the oil. Add the onion, and sauté until soft—about 3 minutes. Stir the chopped chervil into the onion then, using a slotted spoon, transfer the mixture to a bowl and set aside.

In the same pan, sauté the mushrooms for 2 minutes. Remove about two thirds of the mushrooms from the pan with a slotted spoon and combine them with the onion and the chervil. Divide the mixture among four 12.5 cl (4 fl oz) ramekins.

In a colander set over a bowl, drain the remaining mushrooms; reserve their cooking juices for another use. Put the mushrooms in a bowl with the egg yolk and cream and stir well with a wooden spoon.

In a clean bowl, whisk the egg whites until they are stiff. Fold them gently into the egg yolk and mushroom mixture. Season the mixture with the salt and some pepper and spoon it into the ramekins.

Bake the ramekins in the oven until the filling is puffed up, firm to the touch and lightly browned—about 15 minutes. Serve the soufflés immediately, garnished with the fresh chervil sprigs.

Buckwheat Blinis with Caviare

Serves 10

Working time: about 30 minutes

Total time: about 2 hours and 30 minutes

Calories 145
Protein 11g
Cholesterol 85mg
Total fat 6g
Saturated fat 3g
Sodium 325mg

1 tsp	caster sugar	1 tsp	
2 tsp	dried yeast	2 tsp	
300 g	buckwheat flour	10 oz	
¼ tsp	salt	¼ tsp	
35 cl	tepid milk	12 fl oz	
1	egg, separated, plus one egg white	1	
125 g	caviare or black lumpfish roe	4 oz	
500 g	fromage frais	1 lb	
6	spring onions, chopped	6	

Combine the sugar and 15 cl (¼ pint) of tepid water in a bowl and stir to dissolve the sugar, then whisk in the dried yeast until it has dissolved. Add the buckwheat flour and the salt, and mix well, then whisk in the tepid milk and the egg yolk. Cover the bowl and leave the batter in a warm place to rise until it has doubled in bulk—1½ to 2 hours.

Whisk the yeast batter lightly until it becomes liquid again. In another bowl, whisk the egg whites until they are stiff. Fold them into the batter with a metal spoon. Let the batter stand for 10 minutes.

Heat a non-stick frying pan or griddle over medium heat. Drop the batter from a large spoon on to the pan to make little pancakes about 6 cm (2½ inches) in diameter. Cook the blinis until they are golden-brown on both sides—1½ to 2 minutes in all. As the blinis cook, remove them from the pan and keep them hot in a folded tea towel.

Top each blini with a teaspoon of the caviare or lumpfish roe, a tablespoon of the *fromage frais* and a generous sprinkling of the spring onions. Serve hot.

Editor's Note: Buckwheat flour is more variable in consistency than other sorts of flour. When combining it with milk, you may have to alter the quantity of liquid specified here to produce a batter that drops easily from a spoon.

Wholemeal Spaghetti with Prawn Sauce

Serves 6

Working time:
about 15
minutes

Total time:
about 45
minutes

Calories
245
Protein
11g
Cholesterol
35mg
Total fat
7g
Saturated fat
1g
Sodium
290mg

2 tbsp	virgin olive oil	**2 tbsp**
1	onion, chopped	**1**
750 g	fresh ripe plum tomatoes, skinned, seeded and chopped, or 400 g (14 oz) canned plum tomatoes	**1½ lb**

250 g	prawns, shells left on	**8 oz**
3	garlic cloves, crushed	**3**
¼ tsp	salt	**¼ tsp**
½ tsp	cayenne pepper	**½ tsp**
1¼ tsp	chopped parsley	**1¼ tsp**
500 g	wholemeal spaghetti	**1 lb**

In a large, heavy frying pan, heat the oil and sauté the onion until it is transparent — about 5 minutes. Add the tomatoes and 3 to 4 tablespoons of water, and cook the mixture for 15 minutes over low heat. Stir in the prawns and cook for another 5 minutes, then add the garlic, salt and cayenne pepper. Stir in the parsley, mix well, and keep warm.

Bring 4 litres (7 pints) of lightly salted water to the boil in a large pan. Drop the spaghetti into the water, and cook until al dente—about 10 minutes. Drain thoroughly in a colander. Transfer the pasta to a heated platter, then mix in the sauce and serve hot.

Rolled Vine Leaves

Serves 8

Working time: about 45 minutes

Total time: about 2 hours and 30 minutes

Calories 110
Protein 4g
Cholesterol 20mg
Total fat 5g
Saturated fat 2g
Sodium 65mg

125 g	lean minced lamb	**4 oz**
1	onion, chopped	**1**
2	garlic cloves, chopped	**2**
90 g	brown rice	**3 oz**
2 tbsp	chopped fresh mint	**2 tbsp**
1 tbsp	tomato paste	**1 tbsp**
2	tomatoes, skinned, seeded and chopped	**2**
	freshly ground black pepper	
125 g	fresh vine leaves, blanched for 1 minute in boiling water, rinsed and drained well	**4 oz**
2 tbsp	chopped parsley	**2 tbsp**
1 tbsp	virgin olive oil	**1 tbsp**
1	lemon, juice only	
	lemon wedges, for garnish	

In a heavy frying pan, cook the lamb over low heat until the meat begins to release its juices. Increase the heat to medium and fry until browned. Place a colander over a bowl and transfer the lamb and its juices to the colander. Return 1 tablespoon of the meat juices to the pan and sauté the onion and garlic gently in these juices until soft.

Return the drained lamb to the pan and stir in the rice, mint, parsley, tomato paste, tomatoes and some pepper. Add 20 cl (7 fl oz) of water, and bring to the boil. Cover and cook for 10 minutes, then leave to cool slightly.

Preheat the oven to 180°C (350°F or Mark 4). Lay the vine leaves out flat. Place a spoonful of stuffing on the centre of each leaf. Fold the stem end up over the stuffing, fold in both sides, then roll into a small parcel. Do not wrap the parcels too tightly: the rice needs room to expand.

Lay any spare vine leaves in the base of a heavy casserole. Set the parcels in the casserole, packing them in tightly. Pour on the oil, lemon juice and 45 cl (¾ pint) of water.

Cover the casserole and cook the vine leaves in the oven for about 1¼ hours, adding extra water as necessary. Cool the parcels in the casserole. Serve them cold, garnished with lemon wedges.

Indian Spiced Pâté

Serves 10 as
a first course

Working time:
about 20
minutes

Total time:
about 3 hours
(includes
soaking)

Calories
125
Protein
6g
Cholesterol
0mg
Total fat
4g
Saturated fat
trace
Sodium
165mg

250 g	dried black-eyed peas, picked over	8 oz
2 tbsp	safflower oil	2 tbsp
1	large onion, finely chopped	1
1	garlic clove, crushed	1
1½ tsp	black mustard seeds	1½ tsp
1 tbsp	fennel seeds	1 tbsp

2 tsp	chili powder	2 tsp
½ tsp	ground coriander	½ tsp
½ tsp	garam masala	½ tsp
2 tbsp	tomato paste	2 tbsp
1 tbsp	red wine vinegar	1 tbsp
	freshly ground black pepper	

Rinse the black-eyed peas, then put them into a large saucepan and cover well with water. Discard any peas that float to the surface. Cover the pan, leaving the lid ajar, and slowly bring to the boil. Boil for 2 minutes, then leave to soak, covered, for at least 1 hour.

Drain and rinse the peas and place them in a pan covered with water as before. Bring the water to the boil. Boil for 10 minutes, drain and rinse. Wash out the pan, replace the peas and cover them well with fresh water. Boil, then simmer the peas, covered, until tender— about 40 minutes. Add more hot water if necessary. When cooked, drain the peas and

reserve 6 tablespoons of the cooking water.

Heat the oil in a large, heavy saucepan. Add the onion and garlic, and sauté until soft but not browned. Add the mustard seeds, fennel seeds, chili powder, ground coriander, garam masala and tomato paste. Stir well and fry for another 5 minutes. Mix in the vinegar and fry for a further minute.

Process the peas wiht the reserved cooking liquid, until smooth. Stir them into the onion and spice mixture, with the salt and some black pepper.

Turn the spiced pâté into a large bowl and cool before serving.

Terrine of Pigeon and Veal

Serves 20

Working time: about 25 minutes

Total time: about 14 hours (includes marinating and chilling)

Calories 95
Protein 14g
Cholesterol 40mg
Total fat 3g
Saturated fat 1g
Sodium 130mg

4	pigeon breasts, skinned	**4**
6 tbsp	dry Madeira	**6 tbsp**
1 tbsp	balsamic vinegar, or 2 tsp red wine vinegar mixed with ¼ tsp honey	**1 tbsp**
1 kg	minced veal	**2 lb**
60 g	fine fresh white breadcrumbs	**2 oz**

1 tbsp	finely chopped parsley	**1 tbsp**
1 tbsp	juniper berries	**1 tbsp**
2 tsp	salt	**2 tsp**
	freshly ground black pepper	
4	egg whites	**4**
2	bay leaves	**2**

Place the pigeon breasts in a shallow dish and pour on 4 tablespoons of the Madeira and the balsamic vinegar. Cover the dish and leave to marinate overnight in the refrigerator.

Preheat the oven to 180°C (350°F or Mark 4). Combine the veal, breadcrumbs, parsley and remaining Madeira in a bowl. Reserving a few juniper berries for garnish, crush the remainder and add them to the mixture. Season with salt and some black pepper. Whisk the egg whites until they stand in soft peaks, then lightly stir them into the veal mixture.

Place about a third of the veal mixture in a 1.5 litre (2½ pint) oval terrine and press it down evenly in the bottom of the dish. Lay two of the pigeon breasts on top of the veal mixture. Spoon another third of the veal mixture over the pigeon, spreading it in an even layer. Lay the remaining pigeon breasts in the terrine and top them with a final layer of veal. Pour any remaining marinade from the pigeon breasts over the terrine.

Place the bay leaves and the reserved juniper berries on top of the veal mixture. Cover the terrine closely with foil and stand the dish in a large roasting pan or dish. Pour boiling water into the roasting pan to come two thirds of the way up the side of the terrine. Bake the terrine until a skewer inserted into the middle of the terrine feels hot to the touch when withdrawn—about 2 hours. Leave the terrine to cool—about 1 hour—then chill it in the refrigerator for at least 2 hours, or overnight, before serving.

Spinach Fettuccine with Chicory and Bacon

Serves 6 as an appetizer		Calories 215

Working (and total) time: about 30 minutes

Protein 8g

Cholesterol 50mg

Total fat 10g

Saturated fat 2g

Sodium 265mg

375 g	spinach fettucine	12 oz
2	large heads chicory, ends trimmed, leaves cut diagonally into 2.5 cm (1 inch) strips and tossed with 1 tbsp fresh lemon juice	2

5	rashers lean bacon, cut into 1 cm (½ inch) pieces	5
1½ tbsp	virgin olive oil	1½ tbsp
1⅛ tsp	salt	1⅛ tsp
	freshly ground black pepper	

Cook the bacon pieces in a large, heavy frying pan over medium heat, stirring occasionally, until they are crisp—about 8 minutes. Remove the pan from the heat; with a slotted spoon, transfer the bacon pieces to a paper towel to drain. Pour off all but about 2 tablespoons of the bacon fat from the pan, and return the pan to the heat. Add the olive oil and the chicory. Sauté the chicory, stirring frequently, for 2 minutes, then sprinkle it with the salt and some pepper.

While the chicory cooks, add the fettuccine to 3 litres (5 pints) of boiling water with 1½ teaspoons of salt and cook it until it is *al dente*—about 2 minutes. Drain the pasta and add it to the chicory in the pan. Add the bacon pieces, toss well, and serve at once.

Useful weights and measures

Weight Equivalents

Avoirdupois		*Metric*
1 ounce	=	28.35 grams
1 pound	=	254.6 grams
2.3 pounds	=	1 kilogram

Liquid Measurements

$^1/_4$ pint	=	$1^1/_2$ decilitres
$^1/_2$ pint	=	$^1/_4$ litre
scant 1 pint	=	$^1/_2$ litre
$1^3/_4$ pints	=	1 litre
1 gallon	=	4.5 litres

Liquid Measures

1 pint	=	20 fl oz	=	32 tablespoons
$^1/_2$ pint	=	10 fl oz	=	16 tablespoons
$^1/_4$ pint	=	5 fl oz	=	8 tablespoons
$^1/_8$ pint	=	$2^1/_2$ fl oz	=	4 tablespoons
$^1/_{16}$ pint	=	$1^1/_4$ fl oz	=	2 tablespoons

Solid Measures

1 oz almonds, ground = $3^3/_4$ level tablespoons
1 oz breadcrumbs fresh = 7 level tablespoons
1 oz butter, lard = 2 level tablespoons
1 oz cheese, grated = $3^1/_2$ level tablespoons
1 oz cocoa = $2^3/_4$ level tablespoons
1 oz desiccated coconut = $4^1/_2$ tablespoons
1 oz cornflour = $2^1/_2$ tablespoons
1 oz custard powder = $2^1/_2$ tablespoons
1 oz curry powder and spices = 5 tablespoons
1 oz flour = 2 level tablespoons
1 oz rice, uncooked = $1^1/_2$ tablespoons
1 oz sugar, caster and granulated = 2 tablespoons
1 oz icing sugar = $2^1/_2$ tablespoons
1 oz yeast, granulated = 1 level tablespoon

American Measures

16 fl oz	=1 American pint
8 fl oz	=1 American standard cup
0.50 fl oz	=1 American tablespoon
(slightly smaller than British Standards Institute tablespoon)	
0.16 fl oz	=1 American teaspoon

Australian Cup Measures
(Using the 8-liquid-ounce cup measure)

1 cup flour	4 oz
1 cup sugar (crystal or caster)	8 oz
1 cup icing sugar (free from lumps)	5 oz
1 cup shortening (butter, margarine)	8 oz
1 cup brown sugar (lightly packed)	4 oz
1 cup soft breadcrumbs	2 oz
1 cup dry breadcrumbs	3 oz
1 cup rice (uncooked)	6 oz
1 cup rice (cooked)	5 oz
1 cup mixed fruit	4 oz
1 cup grated cheese	4 oz
1 cup nuts (chopped)	4 oz
1 cup coconut	$2^1/_2$ oz

Australian Spoon Measures

	level tablespoon
1 oz flour	2
1 oz sugar	$1^1/_2$
1 oz icing sugar	2
1 oz shortening	1
1 oz honey	1
1 oz gelatine	2
1 oz cocoa	3
1 oz cornflour	$2^1/_2$
1 oz custard powder	$2^1/_2$

Australian Liquid Measures
(Using 8-liquid-ounce cup)

1 cup liquid	8 oz
$2^1/_2$ cups liquid	20 oz (1 pint)
2 tablespoons liquid	1 oz
1 gill liquid	5 oz ($^1/_4$ pint)